*Tune
In,
America.*

TUNE IN, AMERICA.

A STUDY OF OUR COMING
MUSICAL INDEPENDENCE

by

DANIEL GREGORY MASON

Essay Index Reprint Series

BOOKS FOR LIBRARIES PRESS
FREEPORT, NEW YORK

First Published 1931
Reprinted 1969

STANDARD BOOK NUMBER:
8369-1228-4

LIBRARY OF CONGRESS CATALOG CARD NUMBER:
72-90664

PRINTED IN THE UNITED STATES OF AMERICA

This book is dedicated,
in personal friendship and artistic admiration, to
HOWARD HANSON,

who, as first musical fellow of the
American Academy in Rome,
as loyal champion of American music
at Rochester,
as composer of the "Romantic Symphony,"
and as author of "A Forward Look in
American Composition,"
has set up enduring landmarks
along the march of our native musical art.

PREFATORY NOTE

Acknowledgment of permission to reprint matter already published in the form of articles is hereby made to the editors of the *American Magazine of Art*, *The American Mercury*, *The Arts*, *Current History*, *Harper's Magazine*, *Musical America*, the *New Freeman*, the *New Music Review*, and the *Virginia Quarterly Review*.

D. G. M.

"Little Cedars"
New Canaan, Connecticut
June 1931

CONTENTS

INTRODUCTION
xiii

I
THE BACKGROUND
(1900–25)
3

II
AMERICAN MUSIC
(1925–30)
17

III
CONDUCTORS AND PROGRAMS
36

IV
AUDIENCES
49

V

THE VICIOUS VIRTUOSO

60

VI

"ON THE AIR"

71

VII

AMERICA SINGING

87

VIII

AMERICA PLAYING

101

IX

A LABORATORY FOR COMPOSER

114

X

AN OBJECT-LESSON FROM
ENGLAND

128

XI

SOME EMANCIPATIONS . . .

144

XII

... And a Moral

158

XIII

An Æsthetic for America

170

XIV

What Shall We Do About It?

183

APPENDIX

Completing Chapter Two

199

INTRODUCTION

In recent years it has been growing increasingly evident that America is drawing toward the end of her long, necessary period of musical childhood and timid dependence on Europe, that she is even now in the somewhat awkward self-conscious stage of adolescence, and that before long she will be musically adult. Evidence of her slowly reached maturity is to be found all about us: quantitatively in the large new public that has been made aware of serious music by modern inventions; qualitatively and more significantly in the growing interest taken in the work of our own composers, especially by our provincial orchestras it is true, but latterly also by the rather more snobbish metropolitan orchestras and even by Europe itself. Solid documentation for this movement of taste may be found in the epoch-marking address "A Forward Look in American Composition" delivered by Dr.

Howard Hanson in 1925, and in the present writer's *The Dilemma of American Music*.

There remain many difficulties and impediments, chiefly psychological. It is not only that the great majority of our public, as of all publics, is ignorant, easily confused about living issues, and at bottom indifferent to all contemporary experiments toward new beauty; what is worse, the intelligent minority itself is with us over-timid, over-suggestible by foreign prestige, and still lacking in the self-reliance that Emerson urged upon us with such thrilling persuasiveness, yet seemingly so vainly. As for the interpreters, especially the orchestral conductors, with their enormous power to help or hinder, they are divided. Some, of whom Frederick Stock of Chicago is perhaps the most shining example, are heart and soul devoted to our cause, and have advanced it incalculably. Others, of the "prima-donna conductor" type propagated by fashion and commerce, turn a cold shoulder upon us, as upon everything that does not minister to their immediate personal prominence. Our composers themselves, though more technically competent than a generation ago, are not always clear in their own minds what sort of artistic personalities they wish to develop, or entirely able to avoid the pitfalls of economic temptation to triviality, conventionality, or eccentricity.

It is therefore proposed to study in the following pages some of the more important contemporary influences, both favorable and retarding, on this impeded yet hopeful movement toward musical independence. What are the effects upon us, good and bad, of mechanical inventions such as phonograph, movietone, and radio? Do their dissuasion from piano-playing and from amateur participation in music-making generally, and their invitation to passivity and inattention even in listeners, seem to be compensated by their initiation of a new public, their wholesome subordination of the virtuoso as star to the music as art, and other advantages? How are new institutions such as school and college choruses, orchestras, and bands affecting our national taste? What do actual statistics show as to the attitude toward our own efforts of the more professional organizations—above all, of the orchestras—in the various sections of the country?

Finally, attempts will be made to show what further changes, in the public, in interpreters, and in composers themselves, these studies inevitably suggest as desirable. How can each of us, for instance, as a music-lover aware of his participation in forming public taste, make sure that his attitude is encouraging to the further growth of our music? To what extent can the narrower and more egotistic of our interpreters be expected to learn better attitudes, either from the example of their fellows of wider vision or from the increasingly discerning response of a public growing in enlightenment? Above all, what new levels of vitality may we hope to reach as our composers, on whom the welfare of our music most critically depends, advance in maturity of artistic conscience, learn more and more to seek skill rather than influence, to save for technical and æsthetic study energy now wasted in personal propaganda, to give up striving to "overcome sales resistance," instead of mastering the peculiarly stubborn medium in which they have to work? It seems clear that if we can thus use the past to throw light on the future, if we can boldly advance from our present adolescence to a more self-dependent maturity, and if we can all, public, interpreters, and composers, work together loyally for a fine expression that we feel to be peculiarly ours, new things may begin to happen in American music.

Wherefore, tune in, America—tune in and tune up! Be no longer content, as your present habit seems to be, to take your art vicariously, to receive passively whatever happens to be "on the air." It is true that by so listening, to good purpose, you have gained a background, measurably formed your taste, and prepared yourself to make your own contribution. But it is now time to "listen in" in a deeper sense also, to hear not only childishly what your elders have said, but youthfully what you yourself have imagined and dreamed, to try at last your own halting voice, however it may quaver and break, to dare to add to the universal symphony a theme of your own, without which it must remain forever incomplete.

Tune
In,
America.

CHAPTER ONE

THE BACKGROUND

(1900–25)

The charge is often made against our American musical culture that it is artificial and top-heavy, imposed from above by sensitive and public-spirited individuals on a mass essentially unmusical and inert. Our popular music, we are told, is cheap and vulgar, all our good music is made by foreigners and imported. Our own composers, it is said, are imitators and remain nonentities. It must be admitted that there has been some truth in these charges. To illustrate, for instance, from the field of opera, our really spontaneous and indigenous works have been such light operettas as were composed delightfully a generation ago by Victor Herbert, and somewhat less delightfully because more conventionally by Reginald DeKoven, and as are being seductively continued in our own day by George Gershwin. When we tried to be more "serious," as in Horatio Parker's prize opera

3

Mona, produced in the Metropolitan Opera House in 1912, or in Walter Damrosch's *Cyrano de Bergerac* (Metropolitan, 1912) or even in Deems Taylor's highly skilful *The King's Henchman* (1926) and *Peter Ibbetson* (1931), we succeeded chiefly, as someone said of *The King's Henchman,* in "speaking Wagner almost without an accent," but not in being either very spontaneous or in the slightest degree native.

Yet we may truthfully counter the devil's advocate who brings forward these embarrassing facts by adducing the steady and impressive growth, during the last quarter of the nineteenth century and the first of the twentieth, of our musical institutions, such as symphony orchestras, chambermusic ensembles, choral festivals, music clubs, departments of music in schools and colleges, and by insisting that it would have been impossible had there not been beneath it a genuine public interest. And of late we can hardly help feeling that the stage is now at last set for a deeper and more native music expression than we have so far known. America seems to have today all the equipment of a sound musical culture; what we still need is for that culture to get, so to speak, into our blood, to become a part of us, so that we may become musically natural, easy, free from the sense of inferi-

4

ority—in short, no longer merely assimilative, but at length creative. It may be worth while to ask ourselves what grounds we have for these high hopes.

Certainly the period 1900–25 is impressive enough in the matter of the growth and dissemination of the means of musical culture. Most of the symphony orchestras, for instance, of our large cities have sprung up during that quarter-century. Only five have been of continuous importance since before 1900: the New York Philharmonic, founded in 1842; the Chicago Orchestra, started by Theodore Thomas in 1869; the New York Symphony (Leopold Damrosch, 1878); the Boston Symphony, established in 1881 through the wide artistic vision and public spirit of Henry Lee Higginson; and the Cincinnati Orchestra, started as early as 1895 under Van Der Stucken, later carried on by Stokowski, Kunwald, Ysaye, and Reiner, and now under Goossens. After 1900 came rapid development, thus:

Year	City	Chief Conductor
1900	Philadelphia	At first, Scheel. From 1912, Stokowski
1903	Minneapolis	At first, Oberhoffer. From 1923, Verbrugghen

Year	City	Chief Conductor
1907	St. Louis	Max Zach. Recently reorganized
1907	Seattle	Karl Krueger, 1926
1909	San Francisco	Alfred Hertz, 1915–30
1914	Detroit	Gabrilowitsch since 1918
1918	Cleveland	Sokoloff
1919	Los Angeles	Rothwell to 1927. From 1929, Rodzinski

While the older of these orchestras have been maintained largely by endowments from individuals (for example, Boston, New York Symphony, Cincinnati) or by the shrewd and public-spirited business management of small groups (New York Philharmonic, Chicago), the younger ones for the most part depend largely on widespread subscription; and while the precariousness of the existence of some of them may be regarded as evidence of that inertia of our public mentioned above, their existence at all seems to indicate at least a certain measure of practical public interest.

A severer, possibly purer type of music even than the orchestral is chamber music for small ensembles, of which the string quartet is the norm. Naturally, string quartets prosper best under the shelter either of orchestras or of large music schools. Here again the period 1900–25 witnesses a great expansion. Before the turn of the century the only prominent chamber-music organization was the Kneisel Quartet (1886), an offshoot of the Boston Orchestra. In 1903, however, the enthusiasm and intelligence of a New York banker, Edward J. de Coppet, a man with the spirit of a true artist, created the Flonzaley Quartet, which with the Kneisel must always hold in the history of chamber music in America the same fundamental place that in the orchestral field is held by the New York Philharmonic, Chicago, and Boston orchestras. The influence of such organizations is literally endless: it is like the proverbial wave started by the pebble thrown into the ocean, it goes round the world and comes back again. Among more recent quartet groups fostered by orchestras may be mentioned the Chicago, the Cleveland, the Minneapolis, the Verbrugghen, and the Detroit string quartets, as well as the Jacques Gordon Quartet (whose leader left the concert-mastership of the Chicago Orchestra to devote himself entirely to chamber music). Similarly we have the Curtis Quartet, fostered by the Curtis Institute in Philadelphia, the Musical Art Quartet, by the Institute of Musical Art in New York, the Stradivarius Quartet, by the Mannes School in New York and by Mills College, California. Admirable recent

7

organizations that have died for lack of such protection are the Lenox, Letz, and Persinger Quartets. The remarkable movement started by Mrs. F. S. Coolidge in the Pittsfield (later Washington) Chamber Music Festivals has created the Berkshire (later Festival) Quartet, and the Elshuco Trio, named from the first syllables of the names Elizabeth Shurtleff Coolidge.

Impressive by-products of the interest in chamber music are the Society for the Publication of American Music, founded by Burnet C. Tuthill in 1919, and the large amount of space given to American organizations and composers in the *Cyclopedic Survey of Chamber Music*, edited in two large volumes recently (1929) by W. W. Cobbett of London. Writing in this work, Edwin T. Rice of New York mentions the clubs of lovers of ensemble music now forming in many of our cities, instancing the Chamber Music Association of Philadelphia, and remarks: "These may be regarded as typical of the efforts which are now being made to provide assured audiences for the ensemble players touring the country. The maintenance of the various quartets would in all probability be very burdensome but for the support so given."

The development of choral music among us has

8

been perhaps a little less satisfactory. Opera, especially, has always been to us an exotic, and, considering the American irreverence, humor, and cautious matter-of-factness, it seems likely always to remain so. Perhaps that will be no great misfortune, since of all forms of music opera is the most adulterated with non-musical elements, and the least satisfactory. But choral concert music has also failed to show the phenomenal development of its instrumental cousins. The Oratorio Society, the Musical Art Society, and the more recent Schola Cantorum (1908) and Friends of Music lead even in New York a somewhat precarious existence. The Litchfield County Festivals were supported by one man, Carl Stoeckel, and upon his retirement allowed by the participating choruses to lapse. The ancient Worcester Festivals have recently been re-energized by Albert Stoessel, who is also in charge of the new and promising Westchester County Festivals at White Plains. There are successful festivals at Evanston, Peterboro, and other places, and there is the Bach Choir at Bethlehem, again the work of one man, J. Fred Wolle.

Yet, despite the impressive growth of our musical institutions during the first quarter of the century, there unfortunately remained plenty of

truth, at any rate until well into the twenties, in
the pessimists' contention that our culture was a
surface affair, merely laid on from the top, and
that the mass of our people when left to themselves
were either totally indifferent to music or else
frankly preferred its tinsel to its gold. We lacked,
obviously enough, that habit of singing and playing good music for our own pleasure which, practiced however modestly in countries like Germany and Italy (far less in France), gives their
people standards of value, and guards them from
both banality and preciosity. Lacking such standards, our taste was easily corrupted by the first
comer whose commercial interest lay in corrupt-
ing it. It has been shown in the present writer's
"Music and the Plain Man" [1] how the indifference
of the plain people, the central mass of intelligent
Americans, divides our public disastrously into a
thick layer of musical "low-brows" or hoodlums
at the bottom, who support the trivialities and in-
anities of jazz and other "popular" trash, and a
thin but equally injurious layer of "high-brows"
or snobs at the top, who cultivate eccentricity and
fads, thereby dangerously artificializing our concert life. How this lack of a middle body of sound

---

[1] In *The Dilemma of American Music,* by Daniel Gregory Mason.
New York: The Macmillan Company, 1929.

10

taste between the erratic extremes retards the development of our native music has been shown in
detail in another essay, "Our Orchestras and Our
Money's Worth," in the same book.

As for the extraordinary development of mechanical instruments that marked the second decade of our century, and of radio, which began in
the third, its first incidence was undeniably to ag-
gravate the bad influence of the thoughtless and
vulgar segment of the public, by increasing access
to rubbish and inattentiveness to everything.
Quantity production in the pianola, the phonograph, and the radio at first cheapened taste in
music just as, in newspapers and magazines, it
had earlier cheapened taste in literature. Only
after the novelty of such scientific toys has worn
off, and experience with them has made a good
many types of music familiar, does repetition ren-
der intolerable the conventionality, triviality, and
emptiness of the "popular," and increasing understanding reveal the permanent beauty of what
is classic—that is to say, timeless and deathless.
The good thus becomes a touchstone that shows
up relentlessly the actual quality of the bad. (This
is what happened to the farmers who requested the
radio companies to give them less jazz.)

Meanwhile, if one looked to the schools for

relief from the demoralization of this dumping of cheap goods on the public—"education" being our universal panacea—one found, alas, that the school system too was full of its own kind of greed and graft, and that so-called "educators" were actually debauching the minds of our children with fifth-rate sentimentalities and banalities of their own instead of giving them the classics to which tender age and helplessness entitled them. About the middle of the period we are considering, the outlook for the musical taste of the general American public was dark indeed. Well might a friendly German visitor warn us:

"There should be music in every school, and always the best. I do not in the least believe in popular music for the masses; I do not believe there is such a thing as *good* popular music. I think what you call here your rag-time is poison. It poisons the very source of your musical growth, for it poisons the taste of the young. You cannot poison the spring of art and hope for a clear, free stream to flow out and enrich life. You ask me how the American nation shall produce its own music. I say to you from the bottom of my heart that it shall at once cease to train its children with what is called popular music. By this I do not mean that the primitive music of a nation is not the rich, resourceful, inspiring thing; the folk music of all lands has been the beginning of musical culture. But such music as you are producing in America today for the cabaret and the second-rate musical comedy is not folk music. It is just the expression of a restless desire of the people for excitement, for change, for intoxication. . . . This cannot become the source of inspiration for the development of a musical nation. You ask me frankly and I tell you frankly."

Thus Dr. Karl Muck in 1915, shortly before we expelled him as an enemy alien.[1] Yet his brave words were prophetic, and before long we were destined to act on them. For he went on to say:

"Teach your children how beautiful your own land is, and in every school in America teach your children all the beautiful music that the greatest musicians of the world have produced. Have every school one rich chorus, have children sing out all the joy and love of their young hearts. Beyond this, let every school have its orchestra. I do not believe there is a school in America that would not furnish you talent for an orchestra. . . . Oh, you cannot think what this would do for the happiness of youth, for the production of art in this country, what channels it would furnish for genius

---

[1] His article is in the *Craftsman* for December, 1915.

to express itself in the coming generation. And suddenly you will find that you *are* this musical nation that you have talked about, and no one will ever ask again how it can be done and why Americans are not creating music."

Already, at the very time these words were spoken, Dr. Davison of Harvard had struck the first blow for the emancipation of our people from vulgarity by showing that a college glee club could sing truly beautiful music and sing it with contagious enthusiasm. Already, even then, the movement thus started had begun to spread to other colleges through the Intercollegiate Glee Club Association, the first of the concerts of which was held in Carnegie Hall in the spring of 1914. Soon it spread down to the preparatory-school glee clubs, and today it has pretty well renovated our whole conception of choral music. A few years later Muck's vision of an orchestra as well as a chorus in every school began to be realized, in ways we shall later investigate in detail. Thus the first quarter of the century not only provided us with an impressive background of musical institutions, but began the wider dissemination of good taste among our people which is provided by amateur activity of the people themselves, by wisely directed education, and by the intelligent and disciplined use of mechanical instruments.

Yet many people still insisted, as indeed they do today, that all this was a mere body without a head; that, since a living art is measured by its creators, if no one is creating it its apparent life is galvanic, feverish, and unreal; and that in fact we have no original composers of skill and individuality—only imitators and "eclectics." If this charge could be proved against us, it would indeed be a damning one. But in considering it we must first of all make one or two large general qualifications.

Our age is not, we must remember, anywhere in the world, an age favorable to creative art. It is primarily a scientific and an industrial age. We make, Europe as well as America, better automobiles than symphonies. In a short hundred years the change is startling. In Germany, most musical of all nations, Schönberg and Hindemith are a poor substitute for Schubert and Schumann. Modern music has largely lost it naïveté, its sincerity, its emotional vitality. . . . In the second place, America is a bewilderingly large and many-sided country, made up of endless races, groups, classes, points of view. From such a melting-pot it is not easy to distil artistic clarity, and it seems hardly likely that there will ever be an "American school," in the sense that there is a French school, or a Russian, or an English. Admitting, then, that little family likeness can be expected to unite our composers, that they must remain at best oddly assorted individuals, and realizing that we must moderate our aspirations for them and compare them at most with Schönberg and Hindemith rather than with Schubert and Schumann, let us now ask ourselves whether we have as yet any native composers who, with these qualifications, may be said to have established themselves, who justify us in considering our American creative music already a "going concern."

CHAPTER TWO

AMERICAN MUSIC

(1925–30)

To what extent are our native American composers now being played in our concert halls? How well are they surviving the pragmatic test of this actual performance? How far is such neglect of them as may be observed in certain quarters due to their own deficiencies in technique or individuality, and how far is it attributable on the other hand to servility to European prestige on the part of audiences or to inertia, prejudice, or snobbery in conductors? These questions would seem to be worthy the careful consideration of all of us who have high hopes for American music.

At the end of 1925, in an address that promises to become a classic in our musical history, "A Forward Look in American Composition," [1] Dr. Howard Hanson essayed a statistical answer to

---

[1] Delivered at Dayton, Ohio, before the Music Teachers' National Association, December 30, 1925, and afterwards published by the Eastman School of Music, Rochester, New York.

such questions by compiling a "List of Works Performed by the Greatest Number of American Orchestras" during the six complete seasons 1919–20 to 1924–5 inclusive. It is now possible to continue the enumeration for another five years, from 1925–6 to 1929–30; and it is highly instructive to see how far this later list corroborates Dr. Hanson's results, and what modifications and additions it brings to them. The new list comprises American works played in the five years from 1925 to 1930 by the ten leading symphony orchestras of the country, taken alphabetically and each indicated by a Roman numeral, as follows: Boston Symphony, I; Chicago, II; Cincinnati, III; Cleveland, IV; Detroit, V; Los Angeles, VI; Minneapolis, VII; New York Philharmonic–Symphony, VIII; Philadelphia, IX; St. Louis, X.

First of all, let us reprint here Dr. Hanson's original list of the twenty-seven compositions by fifteen American composers which he found to be most frequently played from 1919 to 1925, adding to it, at the right, Roman numerals showing which orchestras have played the same works, and how often, during the additional years from 1925 to 1930.[1]

---

[1] Dr. Hanson investigates "the thirteen most important orchestras of the United States [without stating which], up to, and wherever

FIGURE I

Dr. Hanson's List, with Additional Performances
1925–30

Carpenter:	*Adventures in a Perambulator*. I. III
	Concertino, piano and orchestra. II. II. III
Chadwick:	*Anniversary Overture*
Eichheim:	*Oriental Impressions*. I. II. VI. IX. IX
Goldmark:	*Negro Rhapsody*. I. II. VIII
Griffes:	*The Pleasure Dome of Kubla Khan*
	The White Peacock. IV. IV
Hadley:	*The Ocean*. V
Hanson:	*Lux Æterna*. IV
	Nordic Symphony. I. VI. VII
Hill:	*Stevensoniana*
MacDowell:	*Woodland Suite*
	Piano Concerto No. 2. II. III
	Indian Suite
Mason:	*Symphony No. 1*. I. II. V
	Russians, baritone and orchestra

possible including, 1925–6." Since, writing in December, 1925, it was obviously impossible for him to cover the whole of 1925–6, it seemed best to begin the present list with that year, and to confine it to the ten orchestras mentioned, the programs of which were on file in the New York Public Library.

Mason:	*Prelude and Fugue,* piano and orchestra
Powell:	*Rhapsodie Nègre.* VI
Schelling:	*A Victory Ball.* II. II. IV. IV. VII. VII. X. X
	From an Artist's Life. VII. VIII. VIII
	Fantastic Suite
Skilton:	*Indian Dances*
Sowerby:	*King Estmere.* II. III
	Comes Autumn Time, overture
	From the Northland, suite II. II. VII
	Piano Concerto
Taylor:	*Through the Looking Glass.* II. VI. VII

To this may be added a supplementary list:

FIGURE II

New works, by the same and other composers, of sufficient prominence since 1925 to be played by at least two of the ten orchestras

Carpenter:	*Skyscrapers.* I. I. II. III. V. VI. VIII. IX
Chadwick:	*Tam O'Shanter.* I. II. IV
Gershwin:	*An American in Paris.* III. VII. VIII. X
Gruenberg:	*Jazz Suite.* I. II. III. VI

Hanson: *Pan and the Priest*. II. VII.
                 VIII. X
Mason: *Chanticleer*. III. V. VIII
Powell: *In Old Virginia*. II. VI
Sowerby: *Money Musk*. III. VI
Taylor: *Jurgen*. II. IX
Whithorne: *New York Days and Nights*.
                 IV. X

Taken together, the two lists reveal unmistakably the interesting fact that there exist about twenty-six works, by sixteen American composers, which have been able to hold place, over a period of years, in the repertories of the chief symphony orchestras of the country. No doubt we should be on our guard against attributing too great weight to either the negative or the positive revelations of lists in which so much that is merely local or momentary must of necessity be reflected. The fact, for instance, that all MacDowell's works save the Second Piano Concerto disappear entirely from 1925 to 1930 is probably accidental, and means little or nothing. The great popularity in the same period of Schelling's *Victory Ball* may be partly due to its appeal to after-the-war psychology; that of Carpenter's *Skyscrapers* may reflect in part our momentary industrial-mechanical bias; less favored works may in the long run wear better.

The lists are not offered, however, as affording a basis for any minute or delicately graduated assignment of ultimate values, or even of momentary tastes. What they do show is that a substantial body of American orchestral music exists today, and that it is welcomed and regularly used in our more forward-looking concert halls.

Besides showing what American music is being played, the lists also reveal some significant and possibly unexpected facts about who is playing it—and who is not. Readers who have given no special thought to the matter may perhaps suppose that it is the much talked-of and written-about large metropolitan orchestras of our eastern seaboard, such as the New York Philharmonic–Symphony, the Philadelphia, or the Boston Symphony, that are doing the most to develop our own music. This, however, except in some measure in the case of the Boston orchestra, turns out in the light of the figures to be the opposite of the truth. The Eastern orchestras, more dominated by European traditions and by guest or at least virtuoso conductors, prove to be the ones that neglect our music. Its active supporters are the more healthily local-spirited, provincial orchestras, especially those of the middle West. Dr. Hanson summed up his results in 1925 by remarking that the Eastern orchestras were backward in this respect, probably because many of their short-term foreign guest-conductors "never realize that they have migrated from the homeland," and named as the most progressive in fostering American creative art the Boston, Chicago, Minneapolis, Cleveland, and St. Louis orchestras. In order to see that his conclusions remain essentially true for 1930, all we have to do is to compare a few of the full later lists. Here, for instance, is, on the whole, the best one, that of the Chicago Orchestra under Frederick Stock:

FIGURE III

CHICAGO ORCHESTRA
American works played, 1925-30
(Asterisks indicate first performances anywhere.)

1925-6

Borowski:	*Semiramis* *
Carpenter:	*Concertino*
McKinley:	*The Blue Flower*
Mason:	*Symphony No. 1*
Sowerby:	*Suite: From the Northland*
Stock:	*Violin Concerto*

1926-7

Carpenter:	*Skyscrapers*
Collins:	*A Tragic Overture*
DeLamarter:	*Suite: The Betrothal*

23

Eichheim:	*Burma*
Hanson:	*Pan and the Priest*
McKinley:	*Masquerade*
Oldberg:	*Symphony No. 3* *
Schelling:	*A Victory Ball*
	Violin Concerto
Skilton:	*Suite: Primeval*
Sowerby:	*Medieval Poem,* organ and orchestra
Taylor:	*Through the Looking Glass*
Whithorne:	*Poem,* for piano and orchestra *

1927–8

Carpenter:	*Concertino*
Chadwick:	*Tam O'Shanter*
Clapp:	*Summer*
DeLamarter:	*Psalm CXLIV,* baritone and orchestra
Powell:	*In Old Virginia*
Schelling:	*A Victory Ball*
Sowerby:	*Ballad,* two pianos and or- orchestra
	Medieval Poem, organ and orchestra
Taylor:	*Jurgen*

1928–9

Goldmark:	*Negro Rhapsody*
LaViolette:	*Penetrella*
Norman Lockwood:	*Suite: Odysseus*

24

Sowerby: *Symphony No. 2* *
Stock: *Cello Concerto*

                1929–30
Carpenter: *Birthday of the Infanta*
Gruenberg: *Jazz Suite*
Hadley: *Overture: In Bohemia*
MacDowell: *Piano Concerto No. 2*
Schelling: *Morocco*
Sowerby: *From the Northland*
Stock: *A Psalmodic Rhapsody*
                Violin Concerto
                           Total: 41 works

Remarkable are the hospitality of mind and many-sidedness of interest displayed in this list. Analyzing it, we find three points especially worthy of praise. First, the representation of older or better-established American composers is admirably well-rounded: Carpenter, Chadwick, Clapp, Eichheim, Goldmark, Gruenberg, Hadley, Hanson, MacDowell, Mason, Oldberg, Powell, Schelling, Skilton, Taylor, Whithorne. Second, opportunity is systematically given to younger men: Collins, LaViolette, Lockwood, McKinley, Wald. Third, local talent is regularly represented: Borowski, DeLamarter, Sowerby, Stock. This is an important matter if we are ever to realize the potentialities of our diverse communities in such a way as to establish a vital regionalism at the roots of our native music. Centralization stunts growth; local pride promotes energetic health and hopefulness.

Let us compare now:

FIGURE IV

BOSTON SYMPHONY ORCHESTRA
American works played, 1925–30

1925–6

Copland:	*Music for the Theatre* *
Gilbert:	*Symphonic Piece* *
Spelman:	*Assisi* *

1926–7

Chadwick:	*Tam O'Shanter*
Converse:	*Flivver 10,000,000* *
Copland:	*Concerto for Piano* *
Hill:	*Lilacs* *
Sessions:	*Symphony* *
Steinert:	*Southern Night* *

1927–8

Carpenter:	*Adventures in a Perambulator*
	Skyscrapers
Converse:	*California* *
Hill:	*Symphony No. 1* *
Mason:	*Symphony No. 1*
Piston:	*Symphonic Piece* *

26

1928–9

Carpenter:	*Skyscrapers*
Copland:	*Two Pieces for String Orchestra*
Foote:	*Suite for Strings*
Goldmark:	*Negro Rhapsody*
Hanson:	*Nordic Symphony*
Hill:	*Symphony No. 1*
Jacobi:	*Indian Dances*
Josten:	Two movements from *Concerto Sacro*
Schelling:	*Morocco*

1929–30

Chadwick:	*Sinfonietta*
Eichheim:	*Java,* and *Burma*
Fairchild:	*Chants Nègres* *
Gardner:	*Broadway* *
Gruenberg:	*Enchanted Isle*
	Jazz Suite
Hill:	*Lilacs*
Josten:	*Jungle* *
Piston:	*Suite for Orchestra* *

Total: 33 works

Here again the roster of established composers is impressive: Carpenter, Chadwick, Converse, Eichheim, Gilbert, Goldmark, Gruenberg, Hanson, Hill, Mason, Schelling; and there is a fair proportion of local names: Foote, Piston, Steinert. It is in the younger men chosen that a significant

27

difference from Chicago is noted: Copland, Fair-
child, Gardner, Jacobi, Josten, Sessions, Spelman.
Here the inclusion of such names as Copland, Fair-
child, Spelman (the first a cosmopolitan Jew, the
two latter expatriates) seems to give a more European, exotic flavor—to make the list, in spite of its
New Englanders like Sessions and its New Yorkers
like Gardner, a little less representatively American. At the same time the great number of first
performances tends to arouse our suspicions:
while their presence in moderation indicates a
healthy curiosity and independence of convention,
over-insistence on them may proceed from a precisely opposite pandering to public opinion in the
shape of the journalistic demand for novelty.
Novelty may be sought through motives of sensationalism, while lasting and quiet artistic joy
are compatible only with long familiarity; as Dr.
Hanson insists, "One of the curses of the orchestral
situation in this country is the difficulty of hearing repetitions of successful American works";
and a list rich in repetitions like that of Chicago
may therefore be more truly constructive than one
where "New: First time" appears over-often.

Leaving these doubts in abeyance until we ac-
cumulate further evidence, however, let us turn
next to:

FIGURE V

PHILADELPHIA ORCHESTRA
American works played, 1925–30

1925–6
Gilchrist: Symphony No. 1

1926–7
John Beach: New Orleans Street Cries at Dawn

Eichheim: Burma

1927–8
Carpenter: Skyscrapers

Copland: Scherzo, from Symphony with Organ * (version for orchestra alone)

Farwell: "Once I Passed through a Populous City" *

Gilbert: Nocturne for Orchestra *

1928–9
Chasins: Piano Concerto

Eichheim: Japanese Nocturne

Harmati: Prelude to a Drama

Jacobi: Indian Dances

Riegger: Study in Sonority, for Forty Violins

Schelling: Violin Concerto

1929–30
Eichheim: Java

McKinley: Masquerade

| Schelling: | *Morocco* |
| Taylor: | *Jurgen* |

Total: 17 works

What a striking shrinkage is here! Only seventeen American works in all, as against thirty-three for Boston and forty-one for Chicago! Quality, moreover, is even more important than quantity, and here standard American composers are reduced to a half-dozen: Carpenter, Eichheim, Farwell, Gilbert, Schelling, and Deems Taylor. As for local loyalty, it is given a sop in the shape of a symphony by W. W. Gilchrist; but he died in 1916, and his work is academic and of no significance to our contemporary situation. Among the younger men the only ones whose music has any native quality are Chasins, Jacobi, McKinley. Most of the selections, indeed, seem made not so much for their representative quality or beauty as for a certain piquancy of local color, as, for instance, Jacobi's *Indian Dances,* John Beach's *New Orleans Street Cries at Dawn,* Eichheim's *Burma* and *Japanese Nocturne,* and Schelling's *Morocco,* while in Riegger's *Study in Sonority, for Forty Violins,* the interest in eccentricity is open and unabashed. Shaping this list, that is to say, we find all that love of the bizarre, the strikingly unusual, the journalistically telling—in a word, of sensationalism—which is the weaker but unfortunately the more fashionable and commercially successful side of the great musician (as well as showman) who conducts this orchestra. So well known is this tendency to sensationalism in the policy of the Philadelphia Orchestra, coupled often with indifference to solid but unlurid works, that as one thumbs the programs, one may catch oneself wondering how such a piece as Gilbert's *Nocturne* got into them at all, especially when one reads, in a letter of Gilbert's to the annotator, such a characteristic sentence as this: "I have heard so many of the devilishly clever, uncannily ingenious, but dry and soulless musical concoctions which are all the style nowadays, that I desired to give myself the satisfaction of making an individual protest against all this superintellectual, modernistic tendency."

One reads on, however, and finds the key to the puzzle. The piece was played, as was also that of Farwell, not by the regular conductor, but by a guest, Pierre Monteux. "I did not show the score to anybody," writes Gilbert, "or make any effort to have it performed, but last year Mr. Monteux wrote me from Europe and asked for a new composition of mine for his Philadelphia season, and I wrote back and told him about this. He decided to perform it. That's how it happened." One remembers the sequel. Mr. Monteux, one of the most constructive of all European conductors in his attitude toward American music, was nevertheless slightingly treated by a public and press lukewarm about that music, and after unfortunately losing his temper retired to Europe in dudgeon.

The other two most interesting American novelties, by Chasins and McKinley, were played by Mr. Gabrilowitsch, who was taken to task by the New York *Times* for including in his New York programs a piece which the *Times* considered so "unoriginal" as Mr. Chasins's concerto.

When we observe how adverse to the development of our own music are the influences of the sensation-seeking metropolitan public and the idolized virtuoso conductor, we are prepared to find the programs of the New York Philharmonic–Symphony the least progressive of all. They will be found on the page opposite.

Surely it is hardly unfair to call such a list as this reactionary. The entire representation of American works has shrunk to less than a dozen, of which, aside from those of Ernest Schelling, himself one of the regular conductors of this or-

FIGURE VI

PHILHARMONIC–SYMPHONY SOCIETY OF NEW YORK
American works played, 1925–30

1925–6

| Schelling: | *Artist's Life* |

1926–7

| Hanson: | *Pan and the Priest* |
| Templeton Strong: | *Une Vie d'artiste* (Szigeti) |

1927–8

| Goldmark: | *Negro Rhapsody* |
| Schelling: | *Morocco* |

1928–9

Carpenter:	*Skyscrapers*
Gershwin:	*An American in Paris*
Mason:	*Chanticleer*
Schelling:	*Artist's Life*
Whithorne:	*Fata Morgana*

1929–30

| Wagenaar: | *Sinfonietta* * |

Total: 11 works

chestra, only five are by our better-known men, and only one is brought forward for the first time. In the only year that any adequate representation of even these occurs, 1928–9, only Schelling's *Impressions from an Artist's Life* is in the hands of the regular conductor, Toscanini. Whithorne's piece is played by Mengelberg, Carpenter's and Gershwin's by Damrosch, Mason's by Reiner. The only scores from younger or less known men are Wagenaar's *Sinfonietta* and Templeton Strong's *Vie d'artiste,* the latter included as vehicle for a soloist. In brief, we find here but the slightest interest in the growth of our native music.

To sum up, then, it appears to be amply demonstrated by these lists that the influences making against progress for our music are, first, conductors interested primarily in their own virtuosity, or in the playing, however magnificently, of classic scores, or in propaganda for nations other than those they serve, or in sensationalism either for its commercial or for its fashionable and snobbistic values; and, second, audiences avid of sensation, novelty, and European prestige, or shifting, ignorant, and indifferent, as they are apt to be in metropolises, where the transient element in population is large. On the other hand we see by the example of Chicago that a progressive attitude toward our own music is nevertheless already at work, and working fruitfully, in centres where a steady provincial population of intelligent people is guided, educated, and inspired by conductors of broad sympathies, living ideals, and proportionate musical skill. And these conditions, happily, are more or less duplicated in Cincinnati, Cleveland, Detroit, Los Angeles, Minneapolis, St. Louis, and no doubt in a number of other cities. It is heartening to note that in almost all these cities the regionalism insisted on above finds some exemplification: witness Stillman-Kelley in Cincinnati; Cooley, Moore, and Shepherd in Cleveland; Kolar in Detroit; McCoy in Los Angeles; John Beach in Minneapolis; Kroeger in St. Louis. Even in New York there are Goldmark, Schelling, and Wagenaar. American music has already a habitat. And this habitat is enlarging as our tastes grow less conventional, less sensational, less servilely imitative of Europe—as we learn slowly to be more self-reliant, inventive, and hopeful.

Note: For the sake of completeness in the record, lists of American works played by the remaining six of the ten orchestras studied are printed in the Appendix at the end of the book.

CHAPTER THREE

CONDUCTORS AND PROGRAMS

From the detailed studies we have been making up to this point emerges with painful clearness one highly significant fact—that, much as the interest in our own music among audiences, and its support by conductors, vary over the different sections of the country, both reach a pretty consistent minimum in our greatest city, New York, and in one of our wealthiest and most powerful orchestras, the Philharmonic–Symphony Society. Such a result cannot but give us matter for serious thought.

The programs presented by our leading metropolitan orchestra are necessarily a subject of vital concern to us. On them largely depends our musical nourishment now, and our original musical achievement in the future. For this reason it is not enough that these concerts should be museums of the masterpieces of musical art in the past; they must also be laboratories of the musical art that is to come, and to come here and through us. This point is worth making because, if the museum aspect were all, we might easily feel that Mr. Toscanini's eloquence in the presentation of the classics is so supreme, so nearly incomparable, that all criticism of him on any other score is idle or worse. Thus after hearing from him an almost inimitably beautiful performance of Mozart's *Haffner Symphony,* a musician deeply devoted to our contemporary musical development exclaimed: "A man who can do that need never play a note of American music!" We can all sympathize with that enthusiasm; yet we should not let it make us forget that a conductor, besides re-creating the past, is privileged to help create the future. We cannot, therefore, afford to ignore the increasing body of criticism that a few years ago charged Mengelberg with neglecting American composers in favor of his Dutch compatriots, often of slight talent, and that more recently finds Toscanini showing not the slightest interest in our American future, and even abusing his power by making the new music we hear almost exclusively Italian, and preponderantly mediocre.

During the season 1930–1 an attempt was made to refute these criticisms, so far as they concern Toscanini, by Lawrence Gilman, a critic deservedly admired for his broad and humane culture, his chivalrous fairness, and his disinterested devotion to musical art. In one of his weekly articles in the New York *Herald Tribune* Mr. Gilman abstracted from the programs offered by Toscanini in the period from November 13, 1930 to January 18, 1931 the following list of works. (The figure after the name of each composer shows the number of works by him performed during the period.)

Wagner, 17; Beethoven, 8; Bach, 7; Schubert, 6; Berlioz, 4; Liszt, 4; Franck, 4; Debussy, 4; Roussel, 4; Wolf-Ferrari, 4; Haydn, 3; Brahms, 3; Glinka, 3; D'Indy, 3; Kodály, 3; Sammartini, 2; Rossini, 2; Verdi, 2; Raff, 2; Sibelius, 2; Strauss, 2; Martucci, 2; Tommasini, 2; Cherubini, 1; Mozart, 1.

His comment on this list Mr. Gilman confined to two points. He first showed that the proportion of standard to contemporary works in it is about 4 to 1. This is normal and would doubtless be essentially reproduced in a similar list for any orchestra. The second point concerned the extraordinary preponderance of Italian composers in Toscanini's list. The names ending in the letter *i* number no less than seven out of the entire twenty-five (standard and modern) represented, or nearly one third in a roster of all the composers of the world. And if we take contemporary works only, the disproportion is even more startling—ten works from Italy to fourteen from all the rest of Europe, and America—or, rather, from all the rest of Europe, for there is nothing at all from America. The difficulty of explaining such a disproportion Mr. Gilman evaded rather than faced by his insistence that "Mr. Toscanini gave more performances of works by Wagner alone than of works by all the Italian composers represented on his list." In view of the deserved favor of Wagner with all orchestras and all audiences, the statement does not distract our attention from the Italians, as Mr. Gilman seemed to intend it to do, and even, from a man of his intelligence, seems a little disingenuous.

If we wish, however, to bring out the essential peculiarities of the Toscanini list, the quickest and fairest way is to prepare similar lists for other orchestras. Here are the programs of four representative orchestras in various parts of the country, from the beginning of the season in October 1930 through January 1931—a period slightly longer and more revealing than that to which Mr. Gilman necessarily confined himself.

CHICAGO ORCHESTRA: Bach, 4; Brahms, 4; Wagner, 3; Strauss, 3; Rameau, 3; Gluck, 3; Tschaikowsky, 2;

Schumann, 2; Liszt, 2; Mahler, 2; Franck, 2; Debussy, 2; Ravel, 2; Braine, 2; Handel, 2; Bax, 2. And one each of the following:

Webster, Otis, Rimsky-Korsakoff, Dvořák, Sibelius, Wessel, Walton, Delius, Szymanowski, Schubert, Beethoven, Vaughan Williams, Glazounoff, Borodin, Stravinsky, Wolf, Tommasini, Scriabin, Kodály, Hanson, Stock, Pierné, Weinberger, Rubinstein, Elgar, Szostakowitz, Hadley, Bloch, DeLamarter, Chabrier, Lalo, Bruckner, Chopin, Haydn, Mason, Georg Schumann.

CLEVELAND ORCHESTRA: Wagner, 8; Tschaikowsky, 4; Brahms, 3; Haydn, 2; Mozart, 2; Beethoven, 2; Liszt, 2; Debussy, 2; Ravel, 2; Albeniz, 2. And one each of the following:

Krein, Lazar, Moussorgsky, Mosloff, Shepherd, Schumann, Goldmark, Mondonville, Schubert, Dohnanyi, Bach, Mozart, D'Indy, Lully, Bloch, Strauss, Mason, Chopin, Reznicek, Glazounoff, David Stanley Smith, De Falla, Granados, Weber, Handel, Rimsky-Korsakoff.

DETROIT ORCHESTRA: Beethoven, 4; Wagner, 3; Mozart, 2; Brahms, 2. And one each of the following:

Weber, Rachmaninoff, Hausegger, Balakireff, Schubert, Handel, Graener, Vaughan Williams, Borodin, Wolf-Ferrari, Paderewski, Bruch, Mraczek, Reger, Chopin, Klenau, Hoffmann, Bach, Skilton, Tschaikowsky, Lopatnikoff, Wagner, Mendelssohn, Respighi, Zandonai, Vivaldi, Scarlatti (Mr. Molinari as guest-conductor), Haydn, Franck, Debussy, Ravel.

PHILADELPHIA ORCHESTRA: Wagner, 10; Bach, 7; Beethoven, 5; Brahms, 4; Debussy, 4; Tschaikowsky, 3; Strauss, 3; Mozart, 3; Ravel, 2; Scriabin, 2; Stravinsky, 2; De Falla, 2; Rimsky-Korsakoff, 2; Mahler, 2. And one each of the following:

Franck, Sibelius, Ibert, Bloch, Alban Berg, Zemachson, Cherubini (Toscanini as guest-conductor), Buxtehude, Levidis, Prokofieff, Schubert, Vaughan Williams, Balakireff, Weber, Graener, Borodin, Schumann, Klenau, Mendelssohn, Hausegger, Mason, Bruch, Nikolai.

As one studies these lists, many interesting points emerge. One may learn something from the figures for even the most frequently played masters, by noting, for instance, the preponderance of Wagner on the more sensational lists (Cleveland, Philadelphia), and of Bach and Mozart, Beethoven and Brahms, on those that reflect a finer standard of taste—the Chicago and the Detroit. But our particular interest for the moment is with the least-played rather than the most-played composers: with contemporary and minor composers, that is to say, the choice of whom reveals the presence or absence of breadth of sympathy, catholicity of taste, and loyalty to local enterprise. So viewed, Toscanini's list is seen clearly by comparison to be woefully, not to say ludicrously, lop-sided. In order to include all manner of Italians, from the

41

operatic Rossini and the academic Cherubini to estimable but unimportant personal friends, like Martucci and Tommasini, he excluded most of what is vital and growing in the rest of the world today.

From central Europe he let us hear, besides Strauss, only Kodály (who, to be sure, is worth hearing), and, as if in irony, Joachim Raff, of all people, whose vapid romanticism began to be outmoded at about the time corsets and bustles went out. Among the older men, no Hugo Wolf, Goldmark, Reger, Mahler, or Bruckner;[1] of significant contemporaries, not a note of Szymanowski, Dohnanyi, Alban Berg, or Hindemith. Similarly, from the north only Sibelius; nothing from the older generation of Russians—Balakireff, Borodin, Rimsky-Korsakoff, Moussorgsky, Glazounoff, Scriabin; nothing from the three strikingly contrasted contemporaries Prokofieff, Rachmaninoff, and Stravinsky. From France a little D'Indy, for which much thanks; also considerable Roussel, for which less; no Chabrier, no Lalo, and, virtuosity of omission, no Ravel! From England, as might have been expected, not a note: no Elgar (though Toscanini has played here the *Enigma Variations*,

---

[1] A little later in the same season Mr. Toscanini gave a beautiful reading of Bruckner's *Seventh Symphony*.

as gloriously as he plays most things), no Delius, no Arnold Bax, no Vaughan Williams, none of the just-arriving men, like Walton of the fresh and delightfully British *Portsmouth Point* overture.

But the worst defect of all in Toscanini the program-maker, a defect that in this list seems more than negative, seems almost like positive insult to the country whose guest he is, especially when we bear in mind the prestige of his orchestra as one of the oldest and most honored in that country and remember that it is now the only one in the metropolis, was his total neglect of our American music.[1] So far as his cognizance of us goes, we might never have made any music at all, we might never have made anything but dollars. And alas, so widespread is this view of his, so vastly and dully does our own servility and indifference uphold it, that at this very moment the reader may likely be asking himself: "Well, but *is* there, after all, any American music worth playing?" The answer is that if Stock, and Sokoloff, and Gabrilowitsch, and Stokowski, not to speak of other conductors like Koussevitzky, Reiner,

---

[1] Toward the end of the season Mr. Toscanini included in his programs two short pieces by Abram Chasins, a gifted young American of twenty-seven:—pieces delightfully orchestrated but slight in musical importance—a rather strange choice if he was really trying to give adequate representation to contemporary America.

Verbrugghen, and others, not represented in our present lists, had thought like Toscanini that none of it was worth giving a chance, there would no doubt be little of it worthy of notice today, their belief having tended, as beliefs have a way of doing, to substantiate itself. On the contrary, however, these men took instead, fortunately, a positive attitude; they had "the will to believe," and so helped to create that in which they believed. Thanks to them we have today not only the hopeful experiments of younger men (such as Braine, Otis, Wessel, in our lists), but also a body of orchestral music from such more seasoned workers as Hadley, Mason, Shepherd, David Stanley Smith, DeLamarter, Skilton, and Hanson which can hold its place without apology on any programs. In fact, as our lists testify, this music is in habitual, matter-of-course use on the current programs of our more alert provincial orchestras. It is taboo only in the metropolis of its own country, and there not to the more artistically adventurous if financially straitened groups typified by Mr. Hadley's Manhattan Symphony, but only to the fashion-enslaved, prestige-hypnotized minds that guide the rich and reactionary Philharmonic-Symphony.

For we may as well recognize candidly that it

44

would be both idle and misleading to blame only Mr. Toscanini for the shortcomings of his programs. We shall be ill-advised if we make him a scapegoat to draw off criticism that should justly fall on his employers. His programs could probably be expected to become more representative only through the insistence of the powers above him, since as they stand, they doubtless express his personal tastes. What most interests so great an interpreter of musical beauty is no doubt the most beautiful music in the world—namely, the classics. For novelties he naturally turns to what he is most thrown with, the works of his Italian friends—and we may be sure that politics, in this case, potently endorses friendship; indeed it may well be that he could not come to us at all save as a passionate propagandist for Italian music.

The attitude to be most criticized, then, is by no means his, but rather that of the Philharmonic–Symphony Society, so totally devoid of any American loyalty to match the Italian loyalty that is, after all, rather likable in him. The Philharmonic–Symphony Society tolerates his boycotting of all American music. It accepts at his hands a starvation diet in the contemporary music not only of its own country but of Germany, Russia, France, Spain, England—in short, of all others save only his. It even finances for him with American money an extended European tour in which he plays no single note of American music—and scarcely anyone even notices the fact.

Why does the Philharmonic–Symphony Society act in this way? Not, surely, from any conscious disloyalty or lack of patrotism, but probably from heedlessness, conventionality, and preoccupation with commercial and fashionable, rather than artistic, standards. Since the demise of the New York Symphony as a rival and its absorption by the Philharmonic, this society has a monopoly, and lacks the old stimulus of competition. It can give the sleepiest programs in the world and leave the curious lover of contemporary music no recourse easier or less expensive than a trip to Philadelphia or Boston. Again, New York is a city of transients, of sightseers and sound-hearers—in short, of sensation-seekers rather than music-lovers—and so long as it can see and hear Toscanini, it cares nothing what he plays, and the box-office whose coffers it fills cares as little.

Above all, the controlling personnel of the Philharmonic–Symphony Society is predominantly of the plutocratic psychology and point of view. Now, your plutocrat is peculiarly the victim of fashion or prestige; he, and more particularly she,

cannot conceive that any music without the European stamp can be of any value. The Park Avenue
dowager can hardly be expected to tolerate anything from so near home as the prairies of Mr.
Sowerby or the canyons of Mr. Shepherd's *Horizons*. Such things would be far less safe and edi-
fying than the romantic panoramas of Raff or the
musical millinery of Respighi. There are also,
to be sure, many intelligent persons in the
Philharmonic–Symphony Society, of whom Mr.
Gilman may be taken as a rather extreme type.
That is why it is discouraging to find even Mr.
Gilman ending his article with no hint of dissatis-
faction with Toscanini's list of contemporaries.

All we have been attempting here is a diagnosis
of the serious ailment of the Philharmonic–
Symphony Society in the season 1930–1; we are
not attempting any prognosis as to its probable
future recovery or demise. All we are sure of is
that music is alive today, not in New York, but
in Boston, Philadelphia, Chicago, Cleveland, Cincinnati, Detroit, Rochester, Minneapolis, Los
Angeles, and some other places. . . . Toward the
end of the very period we have been analyzing,
Dr. Artur Rodzinski gave in Los Angeles a concert consisting of the *Sacre du printemps* of Stravinsky and of three contemporary American

works: a program too eccentric to be tried very often, but at least suggesting fresh air to lungs overburdened with Martucci and Tommasini. Almost at the same time Dr. Howard Hanson presented in one of the regular pairs of concerts of the Detroit Orchestra an "All-American Program": not, as he said, from any *parti pris* for programs of this questionable kind, but simply to show people that it could be done. And so well shown were they that musicians, orchestra, public, and even the press hardly commented on the all-American feature at all; they accepted what their ears heard—a group of interesting and stirring modern compositions, effectively scored, provocatively diverse in style and personality. How long is it to be before the Philharmonic–Symphony Society awakens to the fact, patent enough to its provincial fellows, that there is nowadays a large public keenly interested in the living development of contemporary music? [1]

---

[1] The announcement by the society, made just at the time this chapter appeared as an article in the *New Freeman*, of its engagement for a term of seven weeks early in 1932 of Bruno Walter, one of the greatest conductors in the world today and one of the most alert and hospitable to the music of all schools, including our own, seems to give good hope that a more constructive policy is already in sight. In that case the fine old society has in store for it a new lease of life.

48

Chapter Four

AUDIENCES

Children are full of a vitality often inconvenient to adults; and there seem to be, roughly speaking, two opposed methods of dealing with it. The first is the repressive method: "Don't do this"; "Don't do that"; "Children should be seen and not heard." Nowadays this is more or less discredited, as not contributive to the healthy growth of the children and hence, however tempting to the adults, not in the long run serving their best interests. The second is the responsibility-delegating method: "Try it and see"—the method of the "new education," "schools of tomorrow," and the like. As every thoughtful parent and teacher knows, this is much more difficult, laborious, and patience-trying than the other; few things, indeed, require so much patience as to tolerate and even encourage bunglers in the doing, in a roundabout way, by trial and error, of what we ourselves can do easily, directly, and quickly; yet it is a sufficient merit of this that it is the only really fruitful way, for only by trying and failing can anyone learn eventually to try and succeed.

Our American audiences, compared with those of Europe, are childlike, not to say childish. They have the child's inexperience, his timidity, his bashful sense that he does not know and that if he pretends he does, he may give himself away. They have his naïve interest in anything and everything, without much power to discriminate qualities. They have his eager curiosity, especially about the personalities of artists (much less about art itself, which requires more maturity). They have his inclination to like everything, to clap their hands in glee rather than wrinkle their foreheads in thought. Frequently they have even his exuberant physical vitality and consequent tendency to be herd-minded, noisy, and inattentive. What is the best way to induce them to grow up a little?

One of the chief apostles of the repressive method is Leopold Stokowski of the Philadelphia Orchestra. For an ultimatum of his, delivered in an impromptu rebuke to seat-slammers and program-fumblers, most lovers of music will be inclined to thank him. "We must have," he said, "just the proper atmosphere, and we cannot un-

less we have your co-operation. . . . We work
hard all week to give you this music, but I cannot
do my best without your aid. I'll give you my best
or I won't give you anything." This was in Philadelphia at the start of the season 1928–9; despite
the threat in its form, its substance was more positive than negative, an appeal for active co-
operation; and the audience responded with applause (which Mr. Stokowski had not yet banned).
But when, the following season, he turned upon
some—a very few—who had hissed a wearisome set
of variations by Schönberg, and announced that
those who did not care for such music might well
surrender their places to those who did, remind-
ing them that these provided a numerous waiting
list, the feeling was widespread that his attitude
was becoming rather dictatorial and his method
ungracious.

The logical concluding step followed later in
the same season, when he requested the audience
to desist also from applause, as it was a barbaric
method of showing approval and interfered with
the music. Here is the repressive method with a
vengeance. It deprives the audience not only of all
active participation in the artistic experience, such
as might well be thought essential to the healthy
progress of art itself, but even of psychological

and physical relief after the strain of attention.
To sit through a long symphony without any overt
reaction to the music, as Stokowski and a number of other conductors now require, is alike
discouraging to artistic enthusiasm and highly
fatiguing to body, nerves, and mind. After the
Funeral March of the *Eroica,* someone suggested,
Mr. Stokowski might at least have pressed a but-
ton to inform the audience by (noiseless) illuminated sign: "You may now cross the other leg."

By a quaint coincidence, one of the most win-
ning advocates of the other and more modern
method is precisely Mr. Stokowski's sometime
colleague in the conductorship of the Philadelphia Orchestra, Ossip Gabrilowitsch. Discussing
the pros and cons of applause with one of his
audiences in Philadelphia, Mr. Gabrilowitsch,
after paying a cordial tribute to Mr. Stokowski,
who he said was "sincerely looking for a better
way of expression of opinion, and felt that hand-
clapping wasn't ideal," made frank confession of
his own liking for "those countries in the south of
Europe where they shout when they are pleased;
and when they are not, they hiss and throw pota-
toes." He went on to compare our own staid Washington with its more excitable neighbor Balti-
more: "When we play there the next night, you

ought to see the difference. If I didn't know how respectable they were, I should think they were violating the prohibition law. . . . When you like something," he urged, "jump in with both feet and show it." But the most significant idea of all came when he pointed out that the players are artists and need appreciation, and summed up: "It is a mistake to think you have done your part when you buy your tickets."

Musical art, in other words, cannot be bought, but has to be co-operatively, socially created by all concerned: that is a truth that it is hard for our plutocratic and culturally timid America to learn. But since it is fundamental to any genuine artistic life for us, no inconveniences it may carry in its train should be allowed to discourage us from testing it out pragmatically. No doubt if you give children a chance to behave naturally, they will behave childishly. No doubt the "rising vote" proposed by a woman after Mr. Gabrilowitsch's remarks, and given by about a quarter of the audience, was an inarticulate and ludicrously inadequate expression of what was in the hearts of these music-lovers whose possession of hearts had just been recognized. But the point is that unless people, no matter how childish, can act naturally, they will not act at all; and if they do not act, they cannot participate in the artistic experience, since that is by its profoundest nature active and not passive. So, if you want a living art, in the hearts of a living public, there is nothing for it but to bear as best you can the hobbledehoy period such a public has to go through while it is finding itself and coming to mature self-consciousness.

In all ages, of course, it has been necessary to deal with the heedlessness of audiences by one method or another. What seems to be peculiarly objectionable in the repressive or dictatorial method is its standardizing, rigidifying tendency, in an age that is itself too standardized and formal. The issuing of rules and prohibitions to an already over-passive public tends to make it still more negatively docile, if not actually servile. In more creative musical periods the methods of dealing with inattention were more living and human, and as diverse as the temperaments of musicians. Beethoven, disturbed by conversation in a Vienna drawing-room, brushed off the keyboard the hands of the pupil with whom he was playing, rose in his wrath, and left the room, growling: "I play no more for such swine." Liszt surprised the Czar of Russia by a sudden pause in his playing and explained it with a deep obeisance and the remark: "Sire, when the Czar of the Russias speaks, all the world should be silent." Chopin, equally polished, but less powerful and therefore more malicious, replied to the social climber who asked him to play for her dinner guests: "Ah, madame, but I have eaten so little!" But for a nice sense of human fatuity and a pretty indulgence of it, the best example is that of old Haydn. The carefully placed pauses, of two measures each, between phrases at the end of his *Quartet, opus 33, no. 2,* are said to have been inserted on a wager that the ladies would seize these opportunities for talk. One feels fairly confident that Haydn won his bet. And then there is the loud chord in the cradle-song-like slow movement of the *Surprise Symphony,* strategically placed to awaken his London hearers from their after-dinner nap.

The interesting thing about Haydn's method is its recognition of his hearers, its frank and tactful treatment of them as an essential part of the artistic undertaking, even when not a very inspiring one. He knew when they could be depended upon to converse, when to doze off, and even how he could make them laugh, as he does at the end of the *Farewell Symphony* by directing the players to blow out their candles one by one and take their departure. The audience were to him friendly though not over-intelligent companions rather than strictly regimented inferiors, and the healthy common sense and generosity of that conception infused its vitality into his art. Beethoven, too, liked to play with his audience. He opens the finale of his *First Symphony* with a scale that begins with only three notes, and adds one each time it repeats, until it finally achieves completeness and races away into the main theme. It was not Beethoven himself, but one of his conductors, evidently of the Stokowskian school, who feared that the passage "would make the audience laugh," and prudently omitted it. What would happen to Beethoven, we may wonder, if, reincarnated, he were to write a new symphony for Carnegie Hall? Few in that well-behaved audience would dare to laugh with him. The snobs might laugh *at* him, but the majority would doubtless maintain a decorous and owl-like solemnity, and the new symphony would be, so far as they were concerned, still-born.

The apathy of audiences is often explained by youthful enthusiasts, prone to socialistic and radical simplifications, as the response of the dull rich to poverty-stricken genius. "Is it surprising," writes a Columbia student, for instance, in a paper on the development of the symphonic scherzo from the courtly minuet— "Is it surprising that the scherzo has come to express bitterness? Haydn must have loathed all that the minuet stood for when he made a joke of it. There must have been in him a deep disgust at the brainless aristocracy that supported him. Perhaps the bitterness in ——'s new Scherzo is but the result of reflection concerning a democracy that allows its art to be supported by its capitalists. It is at least comforting to hope that there is a desire in today's composers that music shall become truly of the people." One wonders. We may be inclined to agree when we consider the large percentage of Park Avenue dowagers in a Philharmonic audience, the visibly and audibly greater responsiveness to all genuine music of the balcony than of the boxes. On further reflection, however, the explanation will appear too easy and too sweeping. For there is a stupid proletariat as well as a stupid plutocracy to impede the spread of musical intelligence; and a doctrinaire radicalism is as apt to make one insensitive as the dullest conservatism.

Perhaps it might seem nearer the mark to say that in every audience, in all periods, the majority, made up of the dull rich and the dull poor, are inert; but that there is always an intelligent minority capable of taking a responsive and inter-creating part in the artistic experience, and that the far-sighted policy is to encourage this minority to express itself, by every means in our power and at whatever momentary inconvenience. This conclusion seems to be supported by experience in what is possibly the most artistically vital series of concerts given in New York—the Stadium Concerts which take place during the summer. To attend one of these concerts, especially when one recalls by way of contrast the stuffy atmosphere of fashionable Carnegie Hall winter gatherings, is to be electrified by the alertness of conductor, orchestra, and audience, the subtle but powerful currents of sympathy between them, the indescribably joyful sense of participating in the making of art. It is to realize the sober truth contained in this statement of policy in a program book: "If the Stadium programs were by some freak chance to revert to the old-fashioned 'Pop' the Stadium audience of today would undoubtedly disappear. What the audience wants and gets is the standard orchestra repertoire—Beethoven, Brahms, Tschaikowsky, Strauss and Wagner preferred—with a goodly infusion of not too modern modernists. Stadium audiences are interested in music for music's sake, and aggressively support by their continued attendance the program policy which calls for music of the highest order. Popular music at the Stadium means good music. The better the music the greater the crowd."

If our winter concerts could make such claims with the truth these summer ones can, we should be well on our way toward a vital musical culture. And these happy results seem to have been attained by what we have called the responsibility-delegating rather than by the repressive method. A notice issued to patrons during the summer of 1927 is worth quoting, for its intrinsic charm as well as because it seems to sum up with a certain conclusiveness the attitudes of both management and public for which we have been here pleading in the interest of a living art.

NOTICE.

We would respectfully request that the audience refrain from throwing mats. [These are straw mats used to soften the hard stone seats.] While we appreciate and value the spirit and enthusiasm which prompts these demonstrations, in view of the fact that personal injuries have resulted we feel sure that the audience will refrain from this form of demonstration in future.

Stadium Concerts, Inc.

There is an audience for you! How infinitely more promising for the future of American music is an atmosphere of mats than an atmosphere of decorum!

CHAPTER FIVE

THE VICIOUS VIRTUOSO

Radio, the phonograph, the movietone, and other comparatively recent inventions for the transmission of music in quantity have opened up to us such new and bewildering possibilities that it is no wonder if we find ourselves at first a little dazed. The questions of artistic values involved are subtle, far-ramifying, difficult to disentangle; our scientific technology develops by leaps and bounds, while our psychological and æsthetic divination of its implications lags far behind; we thus find ourselves possessed of new instrumentalities of which the effects on our artistic welfare remain more or less undetermined, but which naturally delight our scientific curiosity and profoundly impress our business imagination.

Suppose, for instance, accustomed hitherto only to symphonic concerts of the kind given in Carnegie Hall, we visit the studio in the building of the National Broadcasting Company on Fifth Avenue, whence Walter Damrosch broadcasts for the General Electric Company an hour of orchestral music every Saturday evening. We find ourselves in a large, oblong, high-studded room, brilliantly lighted by six chandeliers designed in modernistic gray cylinders. Their vertical lines are echoed in long gray curtains draped from ceiling to floor, the main purpose of which is to provide admirably complete control of the sonority of the room. On a platform two thirds of the way down stands Mr. Damrosch beside a microphone that receives both his explanatory comment and the music itself. Seated in the larger portion of the hall before him is an orchestra of forty or fifty men; behind him sit invited guests.

Precisely at nine o'clock, at a signal from the announcer, conversation and tuning cease with surprising abruptness, and in the midst of an impressive silence Mr. Damrosch greets his immense unseen audience and begins one of those skilfully made programs for which he is famous. At the point of vantage, just after the opening *Freischütz* Overture, are two movements of a new *Symphony Concertante* for solo horn, piano, and orchestra, by a young American composer, Mark Wessel (who on this occasion plays the solo piano part himself). Such presentation of the work of Americans to their compatriots spread over the continent is a regular feature of these concerts, impressive in its possibilities. After three charming dances from Tschaikowsky's *Nutcracker Suite* have provided relief from the effort of listening to wholly unfamiliar and complex music, there comes the high point of the evening—the entire *Andante* movement from Brahms's *Third Symphony:* in others words, some of the noblest and finest music in the world, played for those who can appreciate it, without inhibition by undue tenderness for the many who cannot. They have their turn ten minutes later, when the concert ends with two delightful dances from *Carmen. . . .* In all this, one is struck by the admirable quality and balance of the sonority, due to carefully worked-out relation between size of orchestra and size and resonance of hall: with about half the players needed for Carnegie Hall, there is more compact and sensitively adjusted tone. We have here, in short, an orchestra of fifty instead of a hundred, playing to an audience of millions instead of three thousand. No wonder the business imagination finds itself inflamed—and indeed, with certain reservations, the artistic imagination too.

On the other hand, these surprising achievements have had, as everybody knows, a ricochet, economic and artistic, singularly far-reaching and in some respects highly menacing. It is no exaggeration to say that they have brought to the profession of music such a crisis as it has never before had to meet. The pessimists, indeed, are already telling us that music is dead, murdered by the machine; more hopeful observers see a new and wider life for it, emerging after a period of readjustment; all agree that the present changes are unprecedented, and the dislocation profound. In 1929, for example, the United States, with a normal purchasing power of four hundred thousand pianos, bought only ninety thousand. In the same year thirty-eight million dollars were spent on phonographs, and eight hundred and ninety million dollars on radio sets. Within a period of two years, between twenty-five and fifty thousand orchestral players are estimated by Olin Downes of the New York *Times* to have been thrown out of work. The Musicians' Union has considered it worth while to run expensive half-page advertisements in New York daily papers, warning the public of "the Robot as an Entertainer" and deploring that the young are being deprived of "all incentive to develop their talent and to make music their life-work." Opera, too, is said to be on the wane. "The lure of radio," says T. R. Ybarra in the *New York Times Magazine,* "the general mechanization of our day, all

contribute to a decrease in opera-house audiences."
As for solo players, Miss Jeanette Eaton presented
their desperate case in *Harper's Magazine* for
January, 1930, using in the title of her article, as
did also Mr. Ybarra in his, the depressing word
"twilight." "There can be no doubt," insists Basil
Maine, a London critic, "that the virtuoso, as we
have hitherto known him, and mechanized music,
as we are beginning to know it, cannot exist side by
side. Yet we must admit that the invasion of mechanized music is inevitable. The virtuoso of old
must eventually be defeated."

To recognize with a healthy realism, however,
the havoc that radio and other mechanisms are for
the moment working upon the living musician,
and especially upon the virtuoso, is not by any
means tantamount to concluding that the decline
of the virtuoso is an unmixed evil, nor that it is
due entirely or even primarily to these devices,
nor, indeed, that their own later effects may not in
some degree correct their earlier evils, especially
if we take the trouble to understand and guide
them. It seems desirable, therefore, to supplement
our first scientific or commercial enthusiasm over
the new toys with a soberer estimate of the artistic
benefits and injuries likely to accrue from them;
and our first step toward drawing up such a

balance-sheet of their deeper human significance
may well be the elimination of certain factors not
really relevant, but likely to confuse us.

To begin with, it is well to realize that in all
periods the virtuoso has been far from an unmixed
blessing to musical art. We find him developing,
through music history, in three well-marked periods, into three striking types: first there is the
prima donna of eighteenth-century Italian opera;
then there is the "wizard of the piano" (or violin)
of the early nineteenth century, a Liszt or a
Paganini; finally there is the contemporary guest
or "prima-donna" conductor. In all three types,
along with real services to music, there has been
much of that vain and cheap exploitation of personality before an empty-headed hero-worshiping
public which is known as the star system and is
notoriously injurious to the art on which it is para-
sitic. The vanity of prima donnas has generated
a whole literature of anecdote; instrumental "wiz-
ards" and boy prodigies have engrossed those gos-
sips who care more for musicians than for music
from the time of Mozart to that of Yehudi Menuhin; and the prima-donna conductors of today
are still usurping much of the attention we might
better be giving to the growth of musical art
itself. Now radio, to give it its due, has two

decidedly salutary effects on those players who think more of themselves than of their art. First, it tends to eliminate entirely a large group of the merely mediocre, the people who have no vocation for music save a desire for the notoriety it may give, or a vague longing for "self-expression," a class who have always been a drag upon it. Second, on the performers it employs it imposes a most salutary absenteeism so far as their corporeal presence is concerned. It removes from the spot-light even that latest virtuoso the guest-conductor, or at least a large part of him, and that the most meretricious, publicity-seeking, and artistically valueless part. It gives us, within limits, his sonorities, his nuances, even his expression (musical, not facial); it happily veils from us his flowing locks, his tailor-made waist-line, his challenging or swooning gesticulations. It makes of us, willy-nilly, no longer spectators, but up to our capacity auditors, and in so doing emphasizes music rather than *tableaux vivants*. An admirer of the *"Liebestod"* from *Tristan,* an excellent judge of music, protests, laughingly but with conviction, that the best performance of it he has ever heard was on a record made by a conductor of such ferocious personal appearance that in the concert hall he had never been able to enjoy his playing. One must in candor

66

admit, to be sure, that should television be perfected, with natural color and stereoscopic relief, Rachmaninoff's hair, cut *à la* convict, would probably again distract from his music the attention of many of his admirers.

A second simplification worth making is to note that while radio has been exerting its influence, for good or ill, considerably less than a decade, the decline of the virtuoso began so much earlier as to be attributable in the first instance to conditions with which the radio has had nothing to do, although, as we shall see, it did later greatly intensify their effects. The actual causes are doubtless many, and highly diverse. On the artistic side there is the decline of singing, and the simultaneous gradual improvement of taste in instrumental music. Psychologically there is the desire of the latest virtuoso, the guest-conductor, to push the others out of the spot-light in order to occupy it himself (in which of course he has been powerfully supported by considerations of expense, especially in view of his enormous salary).

Whatever the causes, a recent study undertaken by J. M. Coopersmith of Columbia University makes the facts singularly plain. Mr. Coopersmith investigated the number of instrumental concertos and vocal arias performed by the Boston

Symphony Orchestra, the New York Philharmonic, and the Chicago Orchestra, in four speci-
men double seasons, 1899–1901, 1909–11, 1919–
21, and 1927–9, representing as nearly as was possible at the time of writing the four decades ending
respectively with 1900, 1910, 1920, and 1930. He
found that arias sung reached their peak at the
end of Decade II (1910) and have since been de-
clining, and that concertos played reached their
peak a decade later (1920) and have now entered
on a similar declination. The sum totals for the
four decades are especially striking when compared with the number of concerts given, which
have increased greatly for all three organizations.
On comparison of the following figures it will be
seen that arias have fallen off precipitously since
1910, and concertos appreciably since 1920.

Decade:	I	II	III	IV
Concertos played:	90	93	160	155
Arias sung:	67	147	120	33
Concerts given:	216	316	433	557

The itemized results are as interesting as the
summaries. Without taking space here to go into
disproportionate detail, it may be noted that of
arias by Mozart there are in the first three decade-
groups six, ten, fifteen; in the last none at all; by

Beethoven, in the first three groups two, seven, six; in the last just one. If it be objected that in any department these classic composers would suffer from changing tastes, we may take the figures for Wagner, who certainly retains to the full his immense popularity: they are fourteen, forty-six, eighteen, eight (and of course we must bear in mind the steadily and greatly increasing number of concerts). As for concertos, here are the figures for the four decades, on the standard piano concertos of Mozart, Beethoven, Chopin, Schumann, Brahms, Franck, Liszt, Saint-Saëns, Tschaikowsky, Rachmaninoff: 19, 21, 58, 38. . . . It is obvious that arias began to give way to concertos twenty years or more ago, and that for at least the last ten years concertos have also steadily lost ground. This means that the concert vocalist is nearly obsolete, and the concert pianist obsolescent.

At this death-struggle of the soloist we cannot, as music-lovers, look on unmoved, especially when we remember that he is only on his worse side the vain showman we have been decrying; on his better side he is also the eloquent artist, the devoted, self-forgetful, and inspired apostle of music. Anyone who can remember the days when orchestral concerts frequently contained the noble and beautiful concertos of Mozart, Beethoven, Schumann,

and Brahms, interpreted with masterly musicianship by players like Paderewski, D'Albert, Bülow,
Carreño, Hofmann, Rachmaninoff, Gabrilowitsch,
and others, can hardly regard their progressive
disappearance with anything but profound sad-
ness. Even the arias and songs of vocalists like
Melba, Nilsson, Jean de Reszke, and Edmond
Clément were of an unforgettable beauty. The
"sensational events" of our own day, formidable
works by Stravinsky or Schönberg played by far-
heralded guest-conductors, hardly make up for
their loss. It cannot, then, but arouse profound
uneasiness when we observe that although this progressive restriction and standardization of the concert repertory began, under the spur of commercial profit-seeking through appeal to the majority,[1]
long before the advent of radio, the effect of radio
has so far been momentously to accelerate and ag-
gravate this restrictive, standardizing process by
which commercialism always impoverishes every
art it touches.

---

[1] See "Our Orchestras and Our Money's Worth," in *The Dilemma
of American Music,* by Daniel Gregory Mason.

CHAPTER SIX

"ON THE AIR"

The formidable first effect of the application of mechanism to music, we have seen, is the impoverishment and paralysis of the living agencies that produce it, even to the degree of a large-scale killing off of the virtuoso, who, as he vanishes, we reluctantly recognize to possess a few virtues along with his many vices. In the very act of saying farewell to this vicious (and virtuous) virtuoso friend of ours we cannot help asking ourselves, with some misgivings, whether the mechanisms which have ousted him are destined permanently to dehumanize our art, or whether, if only we can learn to use and not abuse them, they may yet prove themselves capable, either with or without him, of serving our highest values. Such questions as these are the pertinent ones to ask of recorded music from now on. Its pressing problems are no longer the mechanical and scientific, but the economic, social, and psychological ones. The machines

71

themselves are wonderfully developed; with the advent of electrical recording a few years ago, and of transmission of phonograph records through the radio more recently, the renderings obtainable are immeasurably improved. But for this very reason a deeper study than we have so far attempted or even considered must be made of the psychological implications of these new means, of their incidence on public taste and on demand and supply in music. What we now have to ask ourselves is not what are we going to make of the machines, but what are the machines going to make of us.

Looked at from this point of view, the very vastness of the radio audience which we saw to be so exciting to the commercial mind, is seen to be, for the artistic or humane mind, a matter for apprehension rather than jubilation. To be candid, the commercial and the higher human interests seem to be here flatly opposed. For it is a fundamental axiom that majority taste is always comparatively crude and undeveloped, and that where it is allowed to dominate, art languishes and dies; on the other hand, art survives and grows only where majority taste undergoes that winnowing and progressive refining whereby minority standards emerge from it.

As an instance of this crudity of majority taste

72

one may cite the case of jazz. The features of jazz to which it owes its popularity are precisely the ones that make it most intolerable to a sound taste: its banal melody, its commonplace and sometimes sugary and sentimental harmony, its obvious, over-accented, monotonous rhythm. Now it is interesting to those of us who have high hopes for the future of radio to find that while jazz is still probably the preference of the majority of the vast radio audience, there is already a distinct tendency of that taste to refine itself, automatically, by accumulating experience. A newspaper note that farmers are asking that less jazz be broadcast is highly suggestive. So is the correlative fact that as audiences have progressed in experience more and more good music has been recorded and broadcast: probably two or three years ago Mr. Damrosch would hardly have dared include in his program an entire movement of a Brahms symphony. There seems to be a natural evolution of taste, from fondness for the most trivial jazz and other popular claptrap to appreciation of the great masterpieces, which takes place automatically wherever full opportunity combines with the desire for growth and the strength of mind to concentrate. The great hope in radio is not only or chiefly that it gives this opportunity to more

73

people than have ever had it before, but that for all of them it may prove to carry thus within itself the eventual correctives for its own more sinister immediate tendencies.

As in the attitude toward music, so in the choice of performers there seem to be unfortunate primary reactions, with some tendency to later spontaneous correction of themselves. The first incidence of mass psychology is certainly disastrous. Lack of standards, inattention, indifference lead to uncritical acceptance of almost any performances presented, to tolerance of empty showiness or of mere mediocrity, even to preference of them to more subtle and therefore attention-exacting qualities of interpretation. The result of this lack of fastidiousness in the large public, only too eagerly exploited by the short-sighted economies of producers, is the devastating cheapness of what is called "studio talent." Miss Eaton seems to feel that radio is extending to youthful players in its studios the opportunities of which it is depriving them in the concert halls. But it is a sufficient commentary on the quality of such of these "artists" as she mentions that not one of them is known even by name in the extra-radio world of music, save only Arcadie Birkenholz, of whom it is erroneously stated that he began his career in the

broadcasting studios. And meanwhile many young
artists of real gifts, of fine promise, deprived of
their recital and concert market by radio competition and excluded from radio itself by the under-
bidding of mediocrities or by lack of opportunity
and influence, find themselves obliged to give up
professional playing altogether—to the irremedi-
able impoverishment, let us not forget, of musical
art.

Here again, however, the first tendency is fortunately followed by a reaction. As they hear more
music, audiences become more exacting in their
standards of performance as well as of program and
learn to respond to true musical eloquence and
power. A curious evidence of this maturing process, from an unexpected quarter, may be found
in the increasing favor of what is called "electrical
transcription" (broadcasting from phonographic
records instead of from actual performance). Of
course, the records are cheaper; but it is even more
to the point that when made by trained artists
they are immeasurably more expressive than the
haphazard products of undisciplined "studio talent." It is therefore significant that the new de-
velopments are giving the providers of such talent
serious concern. "Can radio music survive as a
definite art form," asks a questionnaire sent out by

a Chicago firm, "as long as it depends on the grade of amateur talent the broadcasting studios now attract?" (The answer should be an unequivocal negative.) "Statistics show decided increase," continues the questionnaire, "in radio and phonograph combination. . . . Broadcasting chains are more and more using records instead of studio talent. . . . Is it possible that recorded music has, unaccountably perhaps, more 'soul' in it than studio music?" The answer here is that when it has more "soul" in it, this is for no reason unaccountable to anyone not blinded, as producers sometimes are, by economic greed, but for the fairly obvious one that the records are made by better artists; and the inevitable corollary is that the producers may eventually find it worth their while to make a wider and more alert search for talent than has so far seemed to them necessary.

Indeed, as regards both the players and the music used, the crying trouble with our whole radio condition in America is the unenlightened commercialism of its administrators. These producers, stupid men who happen to have achieved a little financial power but have no musical feeling or experience, are complacently unaware that their own taste is far lower than that of at least the more influential minority of their public; they cheapen and cheapen, in their greed for immediate returns, and do not see that they are ruining their own market by underestimating it. They are like their old-fashioned predecessor the concert agent, who, as described by Fuller-Maitland, "is misled by his own preferences, which are generally for the worst type of music . . . and will contendedly face failure for his clients if only he can persuade them to cut out from their programs all that is likely to interest the intelligent part of the public." They are like the managers of the garden café in the quaint anecdote of Saint-Saëns. "One day," he writes,[1] "I was walking in a garden. There was a bandstand and musicians were playing some sort of music. The crowd was indifferent and passed by talking without paying the slightest attention. Suddenly there sounded the first notes of the delightful Andante of Beethoven's *Symphony in D*—a flower of spring with a delicate perfume. At the first notes all walking and talking stopped. And the crowd stood motionless and in an almost religious silence as it listened to the marvel. When the piece was over, I went out of the garden, and near the entrance I heard one of the managers say, 'There, you see they don't like that kind of

[1] *Musical Memories*, by Camille Saint-Saëns, translated by E. G. Rich.

music.'

"And that kind of music was never played there again."

So long as radio remains entirely in the hands of private commercial interests, as it is today in our country, it is hard to see how any substantial improvement over the present degrading conditions can take place.[1]

It cannot but interest us keenly to find that even in England, where radio is organized much more intelligently than with us, being treated as a public utility, difficulties in the music profession such as we have been studying seemed at first, as with us, to be complicated and aggravated by the growing influence of radio, but later were ameliorated by it. There might be a portent for us here, were we perceptive enough to read it. . . . In the fall of 1927 the British Broadcasting Corporation, familiarly known as the B.B.C., the supreme power in the English radio world, and far more public-spirited than our highly divided and competing companies, announced that it would take over the old Queen's Hall Symphony Concerts and give them with a renovated and enlarged orchestra, both the summer season of what are

---

[1] See detailed descriptions of these conditions in articles published by William Orton in the *Atlantic Monthly* during 1930 and 1931.

now known as the B.B.C. Proms[1] and the regular
winter symphony concerts. The keenest observers
of English music, though naturally regarding the
wielding of such immense power by any one commercial company with some apprehension, on the
whole welcomed the experiment as hopeful. "If
things go on as at present," wrote Francis Toye,
"the B.B.C. will soon represent the most important
facet of British music. . . . How can it be other-
wise? They have all the money, they are the only
people who can afford to experiment. Equally important, they have facilities for publicity unob-
tainable by the ordinary promoter. For this reason
—and, be it remembered, I write before the event—
I feel that the B.B.C. Proms will provide, perhaps
for the first time, a satisfactory test of how far London wants good music. . . . If these concerts are
not a great success, I shall despair of orchestral
music in London."

The very first season under the new conditions
(1928), in spite of the fact that some of the
B.B.C.'s innovations were severely criticized, suf-
ficed to prove that the Jeremiahs who expected the
mechanization and the prostitution of music in
England were wrong, and those who hoped for it
a new health as a result of the infusion of fresh

[1] See Chapter Ten.

blood were not far from right. By the end of the second season, 1929, high hopes for future development seemed justified. That season ended, as Harvey Grace described in a letter from London to the New York *Herald Tribune* of October 27, 1929, with scenes of extraordinary enthusiasm. To read his account of the last concert makes an American realize rather wistfully how far our cosmopolitanism is from reproducing anything like the intimate localism, rich in art-nourishing traditions, of a smaller and more compact country like England. The traditional singing of *Rule, Britannia,* the salvo given by custom to each orchestral player as he made his appearance, the time-honored tattoo of heels with which the audience participated in the sailor's horn pipe in Sir Henry Wood's *Fantasy on British Sea Songs*—all these quaint doings seem to set the scene of a country where art is a living experience, and has not been allowed to petrify into a museum piece. At the close of the concert Sir Henry Wood was recalled over twenty times, and as he left the hall and the still cheering crowd in his car with Lady Wood responded laconically with the words: "Till next year!"

Even more remarkable was the concert of the evening before. The program consisted simply of

Beethoven's *Ninth Symphony,* given in its entirety for the first time in the history of the Proms, thanks to the at last adequate financial backing, with the final movement sung by the B.B.C. Chorus. Here was good cheer for those who had been afraid the radio interests would vulgarize the programs; and there was better in the eagerness of the reception. We read that the queue for the purchase of tickets began to form at midday, twelve hours before the concert; that the floor was so crowded that one could literally have walked on the heads of the promenaders; that such enthusiasm had not been shown since prewar days. Here was a sweeping answer to Toye's question whether London really wanted good music, with ample support for his high estimate of the importance of publicity in settling it satisfactorily. An official of the B.B.C. called attention to the interesting fact that the increase in broadcasting from two concerts a week in 1928 to five a week in 1929, far from decreasing actual attendance at the concerts, had notably increased it, the figures for the entire season of forty-nine concerts being 125,000, or about 3,000 a concert. Finally, let the pessimists consider that the Beethoven nights, Fridays, steadily gained in popularity as the season progressed, while the most popular evenings of all, *mirabile dictu*, were the alternate Wednesdays devoted to Bach! It is probable that could radio be taken out of commercial control with us, equally remarkable results might be expected here.

Meanwhile our producers, if they wish their search for performers to be artistically as well as commercially fruitful, must look for talents, however unknown and timid—not for great and blazoned names. The superstitious reverence of our public for such names, catered to by producers for whom standardization is convenient, seems at first sight to contradict its tolerance for mediocrity, but on looking more below the surface we find that both traits come from the same inertness and lack of intellectual curiosity. It is the inability of people with rudimentary taste to judge qualities for themselves that leads them into servile worship of much-bruited names—labels guaranteeing value. Everybody has met stupid people, often of considerable wealth and social position, who recognize no pianists but Paderewski, Hofmann, and Rachmaninoff, no violinists but Kreisler, Elman, Heifetz, and possibly Spalding, no singers but Metropolitan stars, and no music schools but millionaire endowments. This narrow vision, played upon by the herding tendency of business combination and wholesale advertising, brings about a restriction of the field, a denial of opportunity to all but a handful of famous artists, that is one of the most dangerous menaces of radio, and that must be counteracted by more constructive criticism either from within the industry itself or from outside if music is to maintain any vitality and flexibility.

A strong influence in the right direction may be expected to develop from the increasing interest beginning to be taken by the serious music public and by music critics. Mr. Downes of the New York *Times* has begun to touch upon these problems in Sunday articles, and Lawrence Gilman has inaugurated in the *Herald Tribune* a department for criticism of records and broadcasts, happily called "Music's New Gateways." Criticism of this sort, which should increase rapidly, will tend to expose errors of taste and vision such as we have touched upon, and especially to break up the dull herd into intelligent groups. One of Mr. Gilman's correspondents has hopeful suggestions for the direction such educative effort should take. "Because phonograph recording," he points out, "has its mass production side, and much atrocious music is put on record and dinned into unwilling ears, many persons fail to see the difference between its possibilities and the conditions entailed by attempts to reach at one swoop millions of the uncultivated. The difference is that the recording of music for home use at suitable hours and under suitable moods opens the way for fine music to reach its special audiences of one or more under the right circumstances. The effect of recording the best music in the best possible way (which is making progress in spite of comparative unprofitableness and lack of wide critical attention) is the exact opposite of mob appeal. *Mutatis mutandis,* it ought to be possible to work out ways of applying the same selectivity to radio as to records."

It is in such ways as these that we may hope progress will be made by public, artists, and producers in criticizing the mechanical processes in the light of the experience they themselves give, and in thus learning to enhance their benefits and counteract their evils. Such experience will make it increasingly clear that commerce and art make opposite demands at almost every point, and that commerce will have to adapt itself intelligently to art if either, in this type of industry, is to survive. Commerce demands vast audiences, all thinking and feeling alike; art requires smaller groups, united by independent and personal tastes held in common, and each producing a market for the specialized qualities it appreciates. Commerce finds economy in highly centralized administration, exploiting vast territories by routine procedures; art thrives only in conditions of decentralization, development of local talent, free competition. The temptation of commerce is to market great reputations by "national advertising"; but this means, in terms of art, to strait-jacket new enterprise, to reduce everything to the dead level of the already completed, of today and yesterday, to give tomorrow no chance.

Above all, commerce will be obliged to realize sooner or later that all mechanical processes only reproduce and transmit, that living art and artists alone create. These processes should be conceived and administered, therefore, not as substitutes for living artists, still less as rivals to them, but as adjuncts and extensions of their activities. They may increase the range of appeal of music by bringing to it many new listeners. They may refine these listeners up to a certain point by providing them with the elementary musical experiences. They may even, intensifying competition, eliminate among the living players the dead wood, and nerve the serious artists to finer efforts by narrowing their field. But it is essential that a field of some sort should be left them: a field of sufficing scope and diversity of opportunity, open to merit, in which young and unknown artists may develop their talents under valid professional conditions and may make new contributions to art. That is the irreducible minimum without which art must die.

Chapter Seven

AMERICA SINGING

Art is an activity, not a product.

We Americans seem to find it difficult to realize this simple truth, probably because our predominantly industrial life has given us a slant toward estimating everything in terms of production. We are good workers, but poor players and resters, since play and rest require a certain voluntary irresponsibility, not to say contented inefficiency. The amateur does not do things so well technically as the professional, but from his irresponsible and joyous doing of them arises a unique set of values. It is in this set of values that our wealthy and powerful America is pathetically poor, that we are indeed a sort of "poor little rich girl" among the nations.

In our attitude toward musical art, for example, to what extent was the Englishman right who said: "When we English get together for an evening, each one of us sings, dances, tells a story, acts in a charade, or does whatever he can to help amuse the company. You Americans each 'chip in' $20.00, and hire a singer from the Metropolitan to entertain you." Broadly speaking, has he not seized truly the contrast? Is it not a part of our national timidity and self-consciousness systematically to undervalue our own artistic activities and to attempt, by the hiring of professionals, the impossible feat of taking our art vicariously? The sterile conventionality of our concert life in New York, for instance—what is it but the inevitable result of taking all our music professionally, of paying the biggest salaries possible to the most world-famous conductors, demanding of them in return no interest in our local musical life, but rather the effective smothering of any possible faint stirrings of it by the imposition of a "standard" repertory of European music, played with the last degree of technical skill and brilliancy, and with personal "interpretations" sufficiently striking to afford plenty of material for gossip to people too passive and regimented to have any reactions of their own to the music itself? (Of this state of things the European tour of the Philharmonic–Symphony Orchestra, under Toscanini, already mentioned in Chapter Three, was a striking example, almost a *reductio ad absurdum*. Among the flood of press comments, few noted that about this super-orchestra, with its foreign leaders, players, and repertory, there was nothing American but its dollars.)

And what, on the other hand, happens when some especially energetic and enthusiastic musician tries to get up an orchestra of his own to serve a local public? It was tried not long ago in one of our provincial New England cities, about the size of those German cities each of which maintains its own municipal orchestra. When the pioneer conductor, after heart-breaking difficulties in assembling, drilling, and educating his players and firing them with his own enthusiasm, appealed to his local public for their support, their reply was virtually that, since his name was not world-famous (and "nationally advertised"), they were not interested in anything he could give them and would rather spend their money on a single concert of the celebrated X—— Symphony Orchestra, under the leadership of the unique Blank Blanksky, than listen to his entire series. . . . Our system, in short, consists on the one hand of a few professional stars who make all the music and get all the artistic delight, and on the other of a big, standardized, herd public who accept all the labels, pay all the bills, elude all the culture, and miss all the joy.

Out of this practical system spring certain peculiarities of ideology dishearteningly omnipresent with us—certain fallacies we repeat like parrots and erect into added obstacles to any lifegiving approach to art. There is for instance the fallacy that art is something old and queer. This beguiles us into strange crazes such as fads for antiques or for the imitation of the antique, as in Childs' Old England restaurants, or Alice Foote MacDougall's "Venice," "Florence," "Naples," or what not. Some of us even proceed to the fatuity of trying to make our electric bulbs (one of the few unequivocal successes of our age) look like the far-inferior candles of our forefathers. Genuine artistic feeling avoids this spurious and hypocritical regard for mere age and is enterprisingly contemporary. We study the beauty of the past chiefly to help us make more beauty for the present and the future. And after all, our world today has in it much that is beautiful, such as some of our sky-scrapers and many of our motor-cars, power-boats, and airplanes. Another and a kindred fallacy is that art is something far away in space. Europe is "artistic," we are "inartistic": opinions dictated, of course, by our early, not yet outgrown sense of inferiority. Here, unhappily, the superstition tends to induce the fact. What is more pathetic than to see a New York Sunday crowd gape at the Egyptian objects of beauty in the Metropolitan Museum and then go out and scatter old newspapers and empty cracker-jack boxes over their own greensward?

Such fallacies are legion, but all of them proceed from supposing art to be something old, distant, and exotically strange, and not seeing that all vital art is contemporary, local, and as natural as breathing.

This devitalizing separation from spontaneous artistic activities of our own, formerly almost universal, and still responsible for the sterility of our orchestral concerts and other such traditional aspects of our music, is happily beginning to give place nowadays to a more cordial, informal interest in making music itself, a disposition to take it less as work and more as play. Like children long dominated by our elders and by our own timid notion of what is "correct," we are now healthily commencing to throw off conventions and to try things out for ourselves. We are in fact just emerging, so to speak, into musical adolescence. And we are overjoyed to find out what splendid fun artistic activity is, how well within the reach of all normal people it is, and how easily it does what nothing else can do to relieve our tensions, to relax the strains of modern life.

Naturally we are discovering all this first of all through singing, since many more of us can sing than can play an instrument. Practically all boys and girls can learn to sing, except possibly a few so-called "monotones"—and with modern methods of training even many of these. Under expert and sufficiently inspiring guidance they can sing some of the simple but most beautiful music in existence, such as Bach's chorales, the folk-songs of all nations (including our own, derived from the English, and among the most beautiful of all), and the less complicated works of masters from the sixteenth-century Palestrina to the twentieth-century Vaughan Williams. Just that is what our American boys and girls have actually been doing in the last ten or fifteen years, as a result of the school and college glee-club movement so magnificently pioneered by Dr. Davison of Harvard.

There is a story that the Harvard Glee Club, in the early days of that transformation of it by Dr. Davison that has so profoundly affected our whole choral life in America, found itself one evening, after giving a concert in Detroit, in the railroad station with an hour to wait for the train.

After a brief consultation it proceeded to amuse itself—and the waiting passengers—by singing Palestrina. Think of it! Palestrina, not in one of those peaceful medieval cathedrals where his music grew up so naturally, but in the Detroit railroad station! And yet, why not? For in so singing, these Harvard boys were finding three values emerging for them, such as always emerge, in any time or place, when people get together to sing great music.

To begin with, each of them was discovering the value we all find in doing something that appeals to us deeply, and that we can do in coöperation with our fellows, but not alone. This splendid social value was what the schoolboy had in mind who, asked what part he sang, tenor or bass, replied that he "sang quartet." Any good baseball or football player understands this peculiar value of team-work, knows that he is strong not by himself but in loyalty to his group. This social value, of which we always hear a good deal in discussions of the usefulness of choral music to "Americanization" and other such social processes, is in little danger, important as it is, of being underrated. Rather the reverse; for, as we shall see, it ought to remain secondary to more purely artistic values, expressive and æsthetic, and cannot be

93

made primary without defeating them.

Each of these singers was experiencing, in the second place, the relief, reacting through the whole range of his mental health, of giving spontaneous expression to feelings that but for this channel would have remained pent up and repressed. Children know frequently the relief of crying as well as of laughing, grown-ups less frequently, because of what correctness imposes. Swearing can purge the soul, and whistling has often kept a man's courage up. The emotional satisfaction it gives is one of the supreme hygienic or therapeutic values of music, highly beneficial in a civilization which, as ours does, postpones most of its satisfactions (as in the case of everything done for economic motives). Much of our life is drab and immediately unsatisfying. Art presents us with immediate, intrinsic values, and thus calms the nerves and solaces the heart.

The third and greatest value that these singers were finding was the rare joy—painfully rare in a world where, as in ours, there is so much inescapable ugliness—of making something beautiful. Our æsthetic interest is brought to bear on such a bewildering variety of subject-matter in our daily lives that we are prone to lose sight altogether of its presence there and to fancy it held in reserve for special grand occasions. Yet it is omnipresent. The tiniest children like to build blocks into symmetrical shapes, to combine worsteds in harmonious colors, to intone stories in primitive rhythms, sometimes with rhyme. The humblest peasants love a plot of flowers or a bright window-box. Even we, the sophisticated, prefer the commodities we buy to be not only sound and pure, but prepared in pleasing colors, put up in pretty boxes, with the printing nicely spaced and margined. (And though we do not know it, we like sounds to be patterned for the ear in our sentences, like the p's and t's in that last one.) Well-nigh universal is the joy in beauty, that unique joy of which art is only our most purified and concentrated expression.

In Dr. Davison's insight, so fraught with promise to our musical development, there was something of the simplicity of genius. He did not make the mistake of the second- and third-rate men: he did not consent to subordinate the best thing in music, its beauty, to inferior effects such as its social stimulus or its emotional relief. He did not apologize for it or make it a handmaid to something else or attempt to prove its "practical" value by an appeal to commercial motives, or, in short, give any of the thousand bad reasons by which stupid people habitually misrecommend good things. Uncompromisingly he took his stand on its highest value, beauty. People, he realized, whatever their social or emotional releases, cannot take permanent æsthetic satisfaction in mediocre music, such as has gradually sapped the enthusiasm of so many old-type college glee clubs and of the more recent "community singing" movements, any more than they can in mediocre motor-cars or adulterated food-stuffs. He saw that the best in music—which is by no means the same as the most complicated— is the only thing good enough for sound American youth, that Palestrina, in fact, or for that matter Bach, Beethoven, or any other writer of great music, is really just the right thing to sing in the station at Detroit, a city which has nurtured, besides Ty Cobb and Henry Ford, the Detroit Symphony Orchestra and one of the finest art museums in the country.

Dr. Davison and the others active in the movement which eventually embodied itself in the Intercollegiate Glee Club Association wisely made the most of the social motive by appealing to our American instinct for competition. The first intercollegiate contest was held in the spring of 1914, in the form of a concert in Carnegie Hall, New

York. The contestants were Columbia, Dartmouth, Harvard, and Pennsylvania. A few years later a similar group of mid-Western colleges organized a contest group in Chicago. By 1927 the system extended widely over the country. The concert that year was given by the combined glee clubs of Wesleyan University, University of Missouri, Yale, Columbia, Dartmouth, Princeton, Middlebury, Penn State, Furman, Fordham, New York University, Ohio Wesleyan, and the University of California. Olin Downes of the New York *Times* was so impressed that he devoted to the movement an extended article. The interest spread also to the preparatory schools, which formed their own groups and held their own concerts.

From all this activity fresh life has come into our music. Even for the audience a new and more living view of musical art seems to be encouraged by hearing their sons and daughters, nephews and nieces taking part in the production of it. It is brought from cold and distant professional altitudes into the warmer, more intimate circle of everyday life. When we actually see and hear John and Jane singing before us, the deadening fallacy that music is something to be paid for and endured rather than participated in, criticized, and enjoyed

97

is revealed to us in its full absurdity. Mr. Downes, painfully familiar as a critic with the perfunctory and snobbish attitude of the usual Carnegie Hall audience, insists that he has seldom enjoyed an occasion "when the auditors as well as the performers were so earnest and so intelligently interested in what was going forward." He notes that hundreds of letters were received the day after the concert from a vast radio audience, and that their criticisms substantially agreed with those of the judges. And he ends with this impressive statement: "The audience listened and noted the results with an intelligence, sympathy, and absorbed interest in the proceedings not paralleled on the part of any other audience which supports music and opera in this city." (Incidentally, the phrase "music and opera" is worth notice.)

But of course it is the actual participants who gain most in vitality of taste. When a glee club is actually singing from day to day the best music of the world, it banishes from its mind trivial music and snobbish pretentious music as naturally as light banishes darkness. When in addition, as the Harvard Glee Club is in recent years doing, it joins a great orchestra like the Boston Symphony Orchestra in producing masterpieces such as Bach's *B minor Mass* and Brahms's *German Re-*

quiem, it imperceptibly develops an enlightened and cultivated attitude toward art. . . . As these undergraduates grow up, they will unconsciously hold a different view of music from the stupid old one that it was an amusement for the women.

With this changed attitude will go important practical changes. "The American mixed chorus," remarked the critic of a Schola Cantorum concert in New York a few years ago, "still continues to expose what our European critics point out as the prime failing in the cultural life of this country, to wit, that it is mostly limited to the women, because the men, all busied with the job of providing leisure, music lessons and so on for their wives, have no time for it. . . . Every mixed chorus reveals this gulf of the sexes. The women's voices show training, many of them. . . . Not so with the poor men, who are so truly fond of music that they are willing to attend tiresome rehearsals after the day's work. . . . As a rule, the men are inferior save in moral character. Their voices are not flexible. They don't know how to sing. They can read difficult music only with the herd." But nowadays this "gulf of the sexes" is slowly being bridged by the modernized glee clubs; choruses are spreading from the children to the fathers. In the spring of 1930 there was held at White Plains, in the newly built county centre, the sixth annual Westchester County Music Festival. Groups which had been rehearsing all winter in twenty-one neighboring localities were there joined in one huge chorus of nearly two thousand voices. The men, poor fellows, still came in for a few journalistic gibes. A New York City reporter, commenting on excerpts from Borodin's highly colored Russian opera *Prince Igor,* stated that "There were luscious spots and extremely tame ones, for the males that hailed their supposed warrior chief do not drink goat's milk, and they ride not wild horses but New York Central locals." Nevertheless he said of Bach's *Break forth, O Beauteous Light*: "Affording stunning proof of the way the salubrious airs of Westchester develop the lungs, even of commuters, the mighty continuities of Bach were sustained admirably, with effects massive and beautiful too." To this festival a greeting was brought from President Hoover by Secretary Wilbur: "You are to me the pioneers in the great field of organized constructive recreation now so vital to our nation." On the general work accomplished by the Westchester Festival the comment of Percy Grainger was: "I count your endeavor the most life-giving of all the varieties of musical activity known to me."

CHAPTER EIGHT

AMERICA PLAYING

After the young people in our schools and colleges have once formed the habit of singing good music in their choruses, the natural next step is for them to wish to play it also, in orchestras of their own; and this they have actually in recent years begun to do. The animating spirit in this movement is Joseph E. Maddy, founder of the National High School Orchestra. The initial idea was to draw boy and girl players competitively from the high-school orchestras spread over the country and combine them into a single large orchestra for a few days of intensive training and playing. For the first three years, 1926, 1927, 1928, these meetings took place in April, in the cities of Detroit, Dallas, and Chicago respectively, and the orchestra of between two and three hundred young players was conducted not only by Mr. Maddy, but by well-known symphonic conductors who had conceived a lively interest in the movement: Ossip Gabrilowitsch, Howard Hanson, Frederick Stock.

By 1928 it became evident that it would be worth while to organize a summer camp, to which students from all states might come for a month or two of musical experience in common, and the National High School Orchestra and Band Camp came into being at Interlochen, Michigan. Here each summer an orchestra of two hundred, a band of a hundred and fifty, and a chorus of a hundred rehearse two hours daily and give symphony and popular concerts weekly throughout the term. Resident musicians teach individual instruments and ensemble playing. Thirty-four residence cottages, nine class-room buildings, two practice buildings, two clubhouses, assembly halls, and other buildings, including an outdoor theatre seating ten thousand—the Interlochen Bowl—are at the disposal of students. The National High School Orchestra, brought into being in this way, was drawn in 1930 from forty-two states, and consisted of 118 violins, 30 violas, 24 cellos, 23 double basses, 16 flutes, 12 oboes and English horns, 22 clarinets, 11 bassoons, 12 horns, 15 trumpets, 15 trombones, 5 tubas, 9 percussion instruments, 6 harps, and organ. While we are thus marshaling figures, let us add that "all-state" high-school orchestras, and even district and county high-school orchestras, have sprung up as natural feeders to the central organization, until no less than forty-five thousand school orchestras are now said to exist in the United States!

It is inspiring to think what all this means in opportunity to young Americans to get into direct contact with great music—not to "listen in" to it over the radio, but to make it themselves. As the prospectus points out, there is being developed "a system whereby every member of every school orchestra may win his or her way through the various county, state, and sectional orchestras to coveted membership in the National High School Orchestra. . . . No movement in the history of the country," the prospectus goes on to claim, "has ever promised so much toward the musical development of the nation," and adds: "We must look to the musical and artistic development of our citizens for relief from the lawlessness of today which is born in idleness and inspired by the monotony of present-day labor." Fine as is the ideal here expressed, we shall be put a little on our guard by the social rather than æsthetic form it takes, especially if we bear in mind the over-emphasis on the social motive we have seen ruin the old college glee clubs and stultify community singing, and if we note, as we cannot help doing, the quantitative terms in which the movement largely describes itself. What, we shall be obliged to ask at once in the interests of the candid criticism that alone can guide such a movement to its highest potentialities—what is the *quality* of this playing? An opportunity to judge it for ourselves was afforded by a series of six concerts given early in 1930 in Atlantic City, Philadelphia, New York, and Washington. At the Carnegie Hall concert it was at once evident that the creation of a truly musical school orchestra is something much more subtle and difficult than that of a chorus, and that the inclusion of every citizen, however democratically desirable, is certainly æsthetically less likely to lift our society from the "monotony of present-day labor" than to degrade our art to a monotony scarcely less unrelieved. For while almost everyone can sing a little, and the admixture of a few crude singers may remain almost undetected in the mass effects of a chorus, by no means everyone can play, even a little, and an orchestra is so sensitive and transparent a medium that a few unmusical or crude individuals in it can disastrously coarsen its tone and substitute a mechanical stodginess for that living flexibility of rhythm and phrase which is the very life of instrumental music. If you have ever flinched at the relentlessly literal way a youngster will thrum out his accents at the piano, you will think twice before you confide the *Allegro con grazia* melody in Tschaikowsky's *Pathétique Symphony* to the graces of twenty-four conscientious cellos, thirty virtuous violas, and a hundred and eighteen enthusiastic violins.[1]

A problem possibly even more subtle than the adjustment of quantity and quality is that of formulating purpose aright and then always keeping it clearly in mind as the guide to policy and

---

[1] The criticisms of the National High School Orchestra here presented, originally appearing in an article entitled "Our Musical Adolescence," in *Harper's* for October, 1930, and hoped by the author to be constructive and helpful to the movement, have been interpreted, unfortunately, by Mr. Maddy himself, as nagging and unsympathetic, in a reply, "On the Other Hand," contributed to the *Music Supervisor's Journal* for February, 1931. Citing our warning against "subordinating the best thing in music, its beauty, to inferior effects such as its social stimulus or its emotional relief," Mr. Maddy asserts that "in spite of the intolerant attitude of the skeptics, musical participation is now accepted by educators as a great socializing force as well as a universal popular medium for self-expression," and asks: "Cannot social stimulus and emotional relief be achieved through beauty, or are these all-important psychological forces irretrievably wedded to the vulgar and ugly?" The tone of the answer does not encourage one to feel that he has caught the point. One was not denying, but rather asserting, that social stimulus and emotional relief can be completely achieved only through beauty; but one was also insisting (and it seems to need insistence) that if we wish them to be so achieved, we must hold fast the distinction between the three values and never lose sense of the supreme importance of the last. "When half-gods go, the gods arrive."

organization. What is the true aim of the High
School Orchestra? Is it to foster a genuinely amateur activity, in the fine sense of the word "amateur" we have been considering? Is its work to be
undertaken for the direct joy of it, for what it
means in delight and cultivation to the players
themselves? Or is it to be allowed to sacrifice its
unique possibilities by thoughtlessly aping the conventional and commercial policies of the professional orchestras? The program chosen for the Carnegie Hall concert was hardly reassuring on this
point: Tschaikowsky, *Pathétique Symphony*; Liszt,
a piano concerto, with Ernest Hutcheson playing
the solo part; Ernest Bloch, *Epic Rhapsody, "America"*—a totally conventional, routine program, in
fact, such as would form an ideal exhibitory
medium for Toscanini with the Philharmonic–
Symphony or Stokowski with the Philadelphia. But
what sort of program is this to give children playing
for pleasure? How much spontaneous pleasure can
ordinary healthy children take in Tschaikowsky's
melancholy introspectiveness? How can they form a
wholesome taste on Liszt's pyrotechnics and empty
virtuosity? And as for the pompous rhodomontade
of Bloch's *America,* so immeasurably inferior to his
earlier and sincere Jewish works, what normal
youngsters would even sit through it, unless their

æsthetic sense were overruled by obedience or paralyzed by patriotism? [1]

A third problem, and a knotty one, concerns the encouragement of students to play after they have left school. The old stimuli have failed; new ones must be devised. Mechanisms by their competition nowadays disastrously narrow professional opportunities; at the same time they discourage by their superhuman technical perfection the amateur playing which in simpler days did so much to create musical background. "There are now," says Burnet C. Tuthill in a discussion of "Musical Amateurs—

---

[1] This criticism, which is perhaps expressed with undue asperity, Mr. Maddy seems again to take by the wrong handle. "To Dr. Mason," he says, "it is sacrilege for mere children to attempt Tschaikowsky, Liszt, or Bloch. Horrors, they might play a wrong note occasionally!" Of course that is not the point at all; there would be little harm in that. What one fears for is not Tschaikowsky, Liszt, or Bloch, quite able to survive a bit of handling, but the taste of the children who play them. And Mr. Maddy expects to be "censured for blasphemous impertinence." for giving them the César Franck *Symphony*. On the contrary, one could find no nobler music. But indeed, the list of works chosen by various guest-conductors of the High School Orchestra, printed in Mr. Maddy's own article, affords plenty of pieces admirable from all points of view: Schubert's *Moment musical* and *Marche militaire* and Tschaikowsky's *Andante cantabile* from the *String Quartet* (Gabrilowitsch); Dvořák's *New World Symphony* (Stock); Beethoven's *Egmont* Overture (Verbrugghen); MacDowell's *Woodland Sketches* and Herbert's *Irish Rhapsody* (Hanson). All simple, sound music is good; it is the pretentious, the sophisticated, and the over-ripe that should be omitted from a scheme the highest value of which is its gradual formation, through actual participation in performance, of spontaneous good taste.

A Past Reality, a Future Necessity," [1] "1,500,000 boys and girls playing in school orchestras and bands. What is to become of these young musicians when they pass out of school into the business of earning their daily bread?" Mr. Tuthill's suggestion is that they be "encouraged to follow music as an avocation, not to drop it." And he gives a striking instance of a school supervisor in Kansas who, "after successfully developing in the high school an orchestra of symphonic proportions, personally organized from his alumni a civic symphony orchestra which gives a regular season of concerts each year. All this from a population of less than 10,000!"

Student orchestras in colleges and universities should be far more widely developed than they are at present, and no doubt will be as the present young musicians come increasingly from the schools into the colleges, as educators awaken more to the value of music, and as conductors and coaches capable of handling this rather new branch of college work are trained in larger numbers. Already Columbia University, to give an example of what can be done, has a student orchestra of sixty players, including all the instruments, even oboe

---

[1] In *Musical America*, May 25, 1931.

and bassoon. It is organized under the faculty conductor and two coaches, one for the strings and one
for the wood-winds, which ensures a continuing
training and *esprit de corps* from year to year. Only
the best music is played; and so ambitious and familiar with good standards are the students themselves that they insist on programs almost beyond
their technical abilities, but infinitely good for
their souls. One such program consisted of
Brahms's *Third Symphony*, rehearsed with immense enthusiasm and passably played (the rehearsing is of course more important than the playing), a Saint-Saëns violin concerto, with the string
coach as soloist, and the *Meistersinger* Overture.
This sort of thing is the natural sequel of the school
orchestra, and will no doubt spread widely in the
coming decades. So will less formal groups, spon-
sored by organizations for adult education and recreation, especially as the need for a creative use
of our increasing leisure is more and more recognized.[1]

The school-orchestra movement, then, even if
it has not solved all its problems—being still only a
lusty infant—affords both evidence of the musical
renascence that is stirring widely in America, and

---

[1] See the present writer's "Creative Leisure," in *The Dilemma of
American Music.*

promise of splendid future growth. The justice of
Mr. Maddy's claims for it may be cordially con-
ceded. "It will make hundreds of thousands of boys
and girls," he says, "work assiduously for the pos-
sibility of admission to the National High School
Orchestra; it will help other hundreds of thousands
to find themselves in the joy of musical self-
expression; it will lead an appreciable proportion
of our future citizens to recognize the value of music and support musical enterprises; it will do more
toward making America a music-loving, music-
participating nation than all of the professional
symphony orchestras, opera companies, and radio
programs combined." All this is fine, but even better, we must think—even at the risk of being called
"high-brow" by Mr. Maddy—even better is its development of the power of discriminating musical
taste in our children. To them it is presenting the
great music of the world, letting them, so to speak,
shake hands with it and pursue its acquaintance as
they will. The rest will follow automatically. Any
sensitive child who plays the two pieces often
enough will see for himself that Elgar's *Pomp and
Circumstance* March, let us say, though not beloved of the high-brows, is jolly spontaneous music
with which he can have no end of fun, while Bloch's
America is behind its pretentious façade hollow

and empty. The perceptiveness of the young, in this way, once they are introduced to music and left alone with it, is almost uncanny.

Those not actually in touch with undergraduates in our present colleges do not perhaps realize to what a point their enfranchisement and enlightenment in such matters has proceeded. The change since war days is startling. Just after the war a young Columbia man came back from service telling how he had met there a Belgian poet of his own age with whom he had conversed, read, and exchanged confidences, and how he had finally been enabled to throw off his old American shame at confessing an interest in poetry. "Now I am happier than I have ever been," he said. "I am writing poetry, and not concealing it but glorying in it." Everyone over forty is familiar with that old shame of ours at confessing an interest in poetry or any of the fine arts. Many over forty still themselves suffer from it. But to the young today such a view seems hopelessly old-fashioned and queer. They have scrapped such Victorian notions, along with corsets and side-saddles. They sing in glee clubs, play in orchestras, write, sketch, paint, or model in a quite unashamed matter-of-fact way. If you overhear them conversing at dinner, you will find that a play of O'Neill's, a novel of Dreiser's, or a composition of Deems Taylor's is apt to run in and out of their talk as easily and unself-consciously as football or dancing.

A year or two ago a dozen Barnard girls and Columbia boys got up a madrigal club, under the leadership of one of their number. They met from time to time to sing the beautiful old English and Italian madrigals. They had no organization and received no college credit. They simply sang madrigals for their own pleasure, as they might have played contract. The prestige of the glee club in colleges is now quite equal to that of the more ancient traditional literary and dramatic societies; for Harvard's there is a long waiting-list. In at least the leading colleges the student orchestras are beginning to share the cultural enlightenment and the consequent social prestige of these older groups. During the next decade we shall probably see great choral works with orchestra performed entirely, save perhaps for the soloists, by college talent.

And so, now that the youth of the country are thus sensitized to the appeal of music by first-hand acquaintance with it, it seems not unreasonable to hope that our country is beginning to emerge from the crudeness of its artistic infancy and from the self-consciousness and shyness of its awkward age.

AMERICA PLAYING

Perhaps we are even on the threshold of our maturity and about to add the happiness of recognizing and of making beauty to the material power we already possess in such full measure.

CHAPTER NINE

A LABORATORY FOR
COMPOSERS

It is about 10.30 of a winter morning. An orchestra of sixty-five musicians is assembled in Kilbourn Hall, the moderate-sized auditorium, delightful alike to eye and ear, of the Eastman School of Music in the University of Rochester. The occasion is a rehearsal for one of the concerts in the American Composers' Series. Here and there among the empty seats sit three of the four composers represented on today's program, with groups of their friends; one has come east from Cleveland, another west from New York City, the third lives and teaches in Rochester itself. The young man conducting is Dr. Howard Hanson, the animating spirit of the whole enterprise, a man of vision as well as of shrewd practical sense and excellent musicianship, who, while so many of us have been talking about American music, has quietly started this laboratory for the actual production of it. As the

114

rehearsal gets under way, one realizes more and more vividly that this is indeed a musical laboratory. Here is no stuffy atmosphere as of a fashionable metropolitan concert, but a bracing air of adventure and discovery. Here experiments are being tried, enlightening mistakes made, fruitful lessons learned, and the habit established of enthusiasm for art itself, with a healthy disregard of its remote derivatives such as reputation, influence, or money. . . . Over there a composer is jotting down memoranda of passages to be reconsidered when his piece is through playing, from time to time consulting the fellow composer by his side (whom he has met this morning for the first time) as to this sonority or that tempo mark. Presently the other will have his turn to hear just how clearly he himself has been able to imagine that protean monster, a large orchestra. Near the door is their comrade whose work has already been rehearsed, buttonholing a horn-player and beating the time of an elusive passage.

Scene ii.—It is one o'clock, and conductor, orchestra manager, publicity man, and several musicians and officers of the Eastman School have asked the composers, tired but happy, to lunch with them at the Rochester Club. Ten or twelve men sit down together, of all varieties of backgrounds and shades of conviction and taste, musical and general, and proceed to compare notes. The talk, duly sprinkled with badinage and amusing stories, ranges from personalities, up through propaganda, to technical and philosophical questions such as the acoustics of halls, the theory of polytonality, or the problem whether a composer writes for his own satisfaction, for posterity, for an ideal public, for the actual public, or for no public at all. Good stiff blows are taken and received; the introspective idealist confronts reality for at least a glimpse, the compromiser catches some inkling of more daring, forward-looking views, the egotist is heckled, rallied, or hypnotized to a more social standpoint; in short, everybody learns something.

One learns, for instance, interesting details of the actual scope of these American Composers' Concerts, of the rather surprising amount and variety of material that already exists for them. As Dr. Hanson has said in a letter: "The project started as a 'laboratory' for young American composers. For this reason, the earlier concerts contain some works which were in themselves immature, but which were performed for the express purpose of giving the composer the opportunity of hearing what he had written. As the concerts increased in importance and prestige we were given the oppor-

tunity of performing works—frequently first performances—by composers of established reputation. At the present time, therefore, the list
contains a large proportion of America's foremost
living composers." An enumeration of the fifty-one
composers whose works were presented during the
first five years shows the utmost variety in age, experience, and reputation, as well as in æsthetic conviction and point of view: Bacon, Berkeman, Beach,
Boyd, Cadman, Clokey, Copland, Cowell, Delaney,
DeLamarter, Elwell, Gilbert, Hadley, Hanson,
Harris, Howe, Inch, Jacobi, Janssen, Josten, Kaun,
Kroeger, LaViolette, Loeffler, McKay, McPhee,
Mannes, Mason, Moore, Morris, Porter, Riegger,
Rogers, Royce, Rubenstein, Sanders, Silver, Sowerby, Melville Smith, Steinert, Still, Stoessel,
Stringham, Thompson, Tweedy, VanVactor,
Warnke, Weiss, Wessel, White, and Whithorne. . . . What it means for the growth of our
music to give composers of so many types and affili-
ations the opportunity to hear their work, and,
what is more, to give them the sense that they are
members in a living and growing tradition, can be
better imagined than described.

Scene iii and last.—It is evening, and the concert
itself has arrived. An interrupted hum of conversation rises from the audience, made up of the

general public of Rochester, with groups here and there of musicians from the Eastman School who contribute a more personal interest in the affairs of the evening and serve to disseminate information and satisfy curiosity as to the items of the program. So far as applause is concerned, there is the usual amiable tolerance of everything of the familiar American audience; but at the end an interesting experiment is tried, looking toward the development of a more active attitude in the public, more like that of Europeans. Slips of paper are distributed, bearing the typewritten message: "As the Eastman School is anxious to learn the reaction of the individual members of the audience to the compositions performed at these concerts, you are requested to write, on the line below, the name of the composition on this program which you prefer. This is in no sense a competition, and the 'votes' of the audience will be kept confidential." The visitor's impression of the spontaneity and good faith with which the audience entered into their part of the game was corroborated by those who have seen it in longer operation. "The more they suffer," exclaimed one musician admiringly (he was a composer himself), "the more faithfully they come."

The importance of this co-operation of the public can hardly be overestimated. The stagnation of our contemporary American music which the experiment at Rochester is seeking to break away from is the result of a sort of vicious circle of which the two arcs are the sense of isolation and lack of social milieu on the part of the composers, and the bored or actively cynical indifference of the public. Each fosters the other, and between the two no advance can be made except by a few exceptionally resolute individuals, who, with no organic social response to depend upon, waste a large part of their energies and accomplish only the most sporadic results.

Those at all familiar with present conditions know, for instance, how idle it is to expect any interest in contemporary American music from the large metropolitan orchestras of the type of the New York Philharmonic–Symphony. This ancient, rich, and influential society, as is well known, seems to demand no interest whatever from its foreign conductors in the music of the country in which they are working. In his entire term Mr. Mengelberg played very little American music, and that none too carefully rehearsed. Mr. Toscanini has confined himself to pieces by his fellow conductor Ernest Schelling, and to some attractive but unimportant orchestral sketches by Abram Chasins. Mr. Molinari has played no American music at all. And during all the time these conductors from Holland and Italy were so pointedly neglecting our music, they were giving us more than enough good, bad, and indifferent stuff by contemporary Dutch and Italian composers. To resent this policy of theirs, however, is less sensible, and less helpful to us, than to understand it. For them to invest our money in playing us the music of their friends was only natural, so long as we would tolerate it.

The complaisance of the public is thus more to blame than any individuals for the fact that so large an investment of American capital is being used with no interest whatever in the creation of American art; and this complaisance, as we have already seen in Chapter Three, proceeds from the fact that the public of our metropolitan concerts is largely a fashionable public, subject to the peculiar prejudices and inhibitions of its type. The hall-marks of such a public are wearisomely familiar. First, it is more interested in personalities than in musical art; even its hero-worship of a Toscanini is only in small part based on his magnificent musicianship and is largely due to his personal magnetism. Second, it is consequently more interested in performers, in whom personality is immediate and tangible (in short, in those we have called "vicious virtuosos"), than in creators, in whom it

120

is remote or only divined by intelligent sympathy.
How much table-talk is devoted to a great living
composer like Pizzetti, even when he visits this
country, in comparison with that lavished on some
boy prodigy such as Yehudi Menuhin or Ruggiero
Ricci? Third, when such a public does consider
composers at all, it demands that they be composers
of prestige—that is to say, foreign or at least of foreign name. It acclaims an opera-composer named
Giuseppe Verdi, but would ignore one of equal
talent called Joseph Green. Finally, people of this
mentality, or lack of mentality, insist that all music supplied them be of established reputation,
completed, finished, and unmistakably labeled.
The trade-mark must be nationally advertised. An
unknown symphony offends them as *Fanny's First
Play* did one of the critics brought forward in the
epilogue as a type of British respectability: "How
can I tell whether it's a good play unless I know
who wrote it?" . . . Anything tentative, experimental, uncertain (as all things being newly
created have to be) they dislike, as obliging them
to think.

Now is it not obvious that so long as we have, as
one half of our vicious circle, this sort of a public,
preferring any novelty by a third-rate Italian that
Mr. Toscanini chooses to put on the program to

any work, however promisingly indigenous and fresh, even if technically crude, by a man who has the disadvantage of local name and residence, we shall tend to have, as the other half, composers who lack any sense of social solidarity, established function, and *esprit de corps,* and whose technical skill will tend to be insufficient, as too surreptitiously and casually practiced, so that they will frequently, on the rare occasions when we do give them a chance, only confirm our previous opinion that their stuff is raw, half-baked, and boresome? Evidently, if we wish to break this vicious circle, we shall have to resort to either one or both of two correlative reforms. The first is the education of public taste to less conventional, more independent standards—inevitably a long, slow process that must drag on for years before it can show any very heartening results. But there is also the second method—that of developing, within but somewhat secluded from our general society, a group or fellowship of artists, strong enough in their sense of co-operation in a creative venture to ignore the indifference about them—a little niche of yeast, as it were, in the loaf, eventually capable of leavening it, for all its stodginess. Without the sense of fellowship we individual composers are only helpless fragments, overwhelmed with the futility of strug-

gling against the herd and, according to our temperaments, either discouraged, or embittered, or es-
caping to the sterility of the ivory tower. With
fellowship we already have a place, a function, a
loyalty, and a hope. We retire, in that case, not in
the despair of defeatism, but in order the better to
find ourselves and our art, in preparation for eventual conquest of whatever portion of the public is
worth conquering.

That, for instance, is what the reformers of our
drama have had to do. Broadway, like Carnegie
Hall, was too sunk in its commercial lethargy to be
aroused. Habit, routine, the superficiality of popular taste, were too much for it. So from it the little
theatres quietly seceded and began to put on, often
with painful technical crudity, plays worthy the
attention of intelligent human beings, plays that
had something to do with their own environment,
their own culture, their own life. Everyone knows
what happened. Eventually institutions like the
Provincetown Players, the Laboratory Theatre, the
North Carolina Playmakers, the "47 Workshop,"
the New York Theatre Guild, and the little theatres all over the country emerged, new American
playwrights, of whom the supreme example is
Eugene O'Neill, were discovered, and we found
we had a drama, even though Broadway knew

nothing of it.

It may be that our music will have to go through the same process. It may be that public taste will prove too inert and too conventional to foster native music of any vitality, and that our little concerts (possibly largely of college and university orchestras) will have to break away from Carnegie Hall just as the little theatres broke away from Broadway. Or, on the other hand, taste may prove to be transformed more rapidly than now seems possible, under the influence of the provincial orchestras and the general increase of interest produced by the present renascence. Thus we may gradually get a more realistic, contemporary, local, and adventurous policy even in the professional orchestras. . . . In either case it seems clear that a native music can grow up, if at all, only through the efforts of many and most diverse composers, working and studying together in the atmosphere of a public interest not faddish, not devoted to prestige and "success," but open-minded, forward-looking, and hopeful. Hence the good augury of the Rochester experiment.

Postscript. In May, 1931, the tenth anniversary of the founding of the Eastman School was celebrated in a Festival of American Music held at Rochester under the direction of Dr. Hanson, lasting several days and ranging from chamber music and symphonic works to choral works, an opera, and a ballet. On this occasion Dr. Hanson addressed to the New York *Times* a letter explaining the aims and methods of the school, the chief points of which may fittingly be quoted as a conclusion to this chapter.

"Composition is the most important thing in music, and the composer is the hub of the musical wheel. Mr. Onandofsky could not startle audiences with his magnificent reading of the Beethoven *Fifth* if there had not been Mr. Beethoven to write it! In spite of the obviousness of this fact I have been amazed to find that intelligent people were devoting their chief thought to the performer rather than to the creator.

"As the composer is of prime importance in music, so is the national composer important in the development of a national musical culture. The development of the 'Russian school' is of recent enough date to serve as a striking example. There is no reason to believe that the United States is an exception to this general law of development, nor is there any reason to believe that we shall develop our own music except by the same intense concentration upon our own composers.

"It is not possible for one man, no matter how great he may be, to produce a significant national development. Such a development must be the work of many composers. Some of these men will have great talent and some will be of lesser talent, but it will be the combined efforts of all these men that will be fruitful.

"It is equally imperative to foster spiritual atmosphere that is favorable to creation. In other words, the subsoil must also be tilled so that we develop among those interested in music a feeling of interest in and sympathy toward creation. I believe that this is a matter of the greatest importance. It is a problem of back-breaking difficulty for a composer, no matter how great his talent, to attempt to express himself if he is living in an atmosphere where his fellow men and women have no interest in or sympathy toward what he is doing and do not consider that it would be important even if he should produce a masterpiece! I believe that even a Beethoven might conceivably be frustrated in such an environment.

"These concerts have been generally attended by the composers whose works were performed, and out of this has come an important and rather unexpected development. Composers from all over the country have gathered together from time to time and have come to know each other. They have discussed their problems and their philosophies of music and in doing so have developed a sympathetic understanding of one another. They have found that the American composer is trying to do a distinctive piece of work in expressing through music the life of his own country. This resulted in a certain consolidation of purpose, a sort of communism of artistic endeavor, which has been very thrilling for me to watch.

"The festival of American music which we have just concluded called forth from the entire faculty and the student body the greatest zeal and enthusiasm. It is impossible to live in the midst of such an atmosphere without feeling its stimulus and essential productivity."

CHAPTER TEN

AN OBJECT-LESSON FROM
ENGLAND

To an American music-lover even a casual attendance at the Promenade Concerts, or "Proms,"
given in Queen's Hall during the London summer season is provocative of thought; to an American composer of optimistic temperament it cannot
fail to be exciting, while to a pessimist it may well,
like Wordsworth's primrose, suggest "thoughts
that do often lie too deep for tears."

For here, to begin with, are concerts highly successful without recourse to the appeal, so taken for
granted with us, to virtuosity, showmanship, and
in extreme cases charlatanism, in the conductor.
During no less than thirty-six years Sir Henry
Wood has conducted these concerts with admirable skill and authority and, as anyone familiar
with New York methods could not but notice,
with an almost more admirable absence of pose
and self-importance. He is a conductor who makes

it clear at once that he intends to play, not on the audience's hero-worship and love of sensation, but on the orchestra as a musical instrument; that he has selected his program not to show himself off, but to set together various and effectively contrasting types of beauty; [1] that to even the virtuosos—in spite of their inevitably distracting attention from him—he is disposed to give their chance by including in his scheme both instrumental concertos and vocal arias, now nearly obsolete in New York.

And his audiences respond to this treatment of them as mature human beings rather than gaping children, as most audiences will if given the chance, with intelligent and on occasion with intense interest. The listeners at the Proms, in their alertness, their air of participating actively in the artistic experience, remind an American of the Stadium rather than of the Carnegie Hall public, with its fads, its snobberies, and its boredoms. To hear these Englishmen, conventionally supposed to be undemonstrative, bursting into cheers at the end of a piece, and that not a concerto but a symphony,

---

[1] In his younger days, we may surmise from the comment of Fuller-Maitland to be quoted in the next chapter, he was perhaps a little less disinterested and more *poseur*—more like the prima-donna conductor type so painfully familiar to us on this side. But experience has ripened him.

and a symphony by a native composer, and insisting on recalling over and over again this composer to the stage, thrilling him with the realization that he has written, not notes on paper, but thoughts and feelings finding echo in the hearts of his fellows, is to awaken to what music in America also might be if it could only be guided a little more by intelligence and artistic enthusiasm, a little less by fashion, routine, and the box-office.

The present hopeful stage in the long career of the Proms has not been attained without some vicissitudes. Orchestral music in London has for years been in a condition fluctuating from unsatisfactory to precarious, owing primarily to inadequate financial support, secondarily to lax standards of performance and to certain abuses too long tolerated. For sheer technical excellence, for brilliance and beauty of tone and finish of execution, the London Symphony Orchestra has never equalled such American super-orchestras as the Philadelphia, the Boston, and perhaps the New York Philharmonic–Symphony. The whole traditional approach to music has been different. There has been less rehearsing than with us and far less concentration on technical finish (with its often unnoted concomitant of limitation of repertory). No doubt the weakness has been toleration of sloppy playing. An English orchestra, it has been jestingly said, can read anything, but can never do more with anything than read it. On the other hand, we pay too high a price for our technical excellence, in reactionary conventionality of programs (as we have seen in considerable detail in the earlier chapters of this book), to throw stones at those who prefer more living qualities; and it might be said that if our American orchestras go much further in their present direction, they will not need to be able to read at all, but can devote themselves to learning by rote and playing over and over again, with impeccable skill and no glimmer of artistic adventure, a dozen "war-horses" such as Tschaikowsky's *Pathétique Symphony,* Liszt's *Les Préludes,* and Rimsky-Korsakoff's *Scheherezade.*

From our present point of view, the most suggestive feature of the English freedom and variety of repertory is the regular inclusion of contemporary British music in the programs of the Proms. The plan of setting aside Thursday evenings of each week for British composers, initiated along with other reforms when the British Broadcasting Corporation took over these concerts in 1927,[1]

---

[1] See Chapter Six for more general considerations on the effect of radio on music in England.

did not, it is true, escape a good deal of adverse criticism. Dr. Vaughan Williams made himself the spokesman of his fellow composers in a letter to *The Times* protesting against the "segregation" of English music and pleading for its inclusion as a matter of course in general programs—an attitude that will remind Americans of MacDowell's actual withdrawal of one of his compositions from an "All-American program." In private conversation Dr. Vaughan Williams later supplemented this argument with another based rather on consideration for the public. "Some of these people," he said with a wry smile, "have to think twice before they spend their scanty shillings. Why should they be expected to choose Thursday evenings, and listen to a lot of unfamiliar stuff, good, bad, and indifferent, instead of Mondays, Wednesdays, or Fridays when they can hear some old favorites they have good reason to love?" (New Yorkers will recall a piano recital of Josef Hofmann's in Carnegie Hall some years ago, ostensibly devoted entirely to American compositions, but in effect rather giving them all a black eye by the simple device of concluding with a few encore pieces from Chopin. Nationalism can be a knife that cuts both ways.)

Yet that these British Composers' Nights on the

whole bore well the pragmatic test, anyone who had the privilege of hearing some of them during the summer of 1930 will probably agree. In the two Thursday evenings August 14th and 21st, for example, while one undoubtedly had to sit through some boresome compositions, the whole experience was admirably worth while for the sake of two splendid symphonies that would bear comparison with those of any contemporary school: Arnold Bax's *First Symphony, in E flat minor,* and Vaughan Williams's *Pastoral Symphony.*

Bax's music has undergone a curious evolution from extreme complexity to comparative or at least increasing simplicity. A brilliant youth, famous at the Royal Academy of Music for his uncanny power of reading the most complicated scores at sight, Bax's characteristic fault was turgidity and over-elaboration. In his *First Symphony* there is a good deal of overwriting, and there are too many ideas and a lack of directness. The *Third,* dedicated to Sir Henry Wood, is said to be a great advance in these respects. But even in the *First,* besides an orchestral brilliancy and effectiveness unusual even today, there is a boldness of thought and feeling, a sturdy self-reliance, that are always rare and that make the work deeply impressive. This directness of appeal it was that reached the hearts of the audience and aroused that storm of applause mingled with shouts when the composer appeared on the stage, referred to already as the kind of thing that makes music come alive in any nation.

Dr. Vaughan Williams conducted his own symphony. It is a beautiful work, that somehow manages by a reticent and suggestive method, without any pother and without any overt references, to arouse all one's associations of the quiet gray-and-green landscape of English fields, and of the reticent but kindly feeling of English people. An elusive work that as little wears its heart on its sleeve as its shy and not over-articulate composer in a casual meeting (Vaughan Williams has as little small talk as big talk, though he can talk enlighteningly on what interests him), it is hard to say why it makes so deep an impression of something quintessentially English. Not especially English, certainly, is the harmonic manner—one would rather say modern French impressionist in its clamping together of triads that move about as wholes like those of Debussy or Ravel, an idiom that in its unchangingness seems sometimes to verge on automatism. While melodically there are traces of folk-song, what seems more directly productive of the deep emotional appeal is a sort of hypnotic insistence on very quiet, almost drab, but wondrously imaginative and magical instrumental refrains: the poetic soliloquy of the English horn in the first movement; in the second, the E-flat trumpet with its monotonous obbligato in its natural series of overtones, with the dreamlike "flat seventh"—a tone usually modified to conform to our artificial system; the delicious celesta passage at the end of the Scherzo; above all, that unique, that unforgettable effect of the solo soprano, distant, wordless, at the beginning of the finale and again at its end. At the beginning, with masterly economy, it is accompanied only by a drum roll; at the end by long-held high unisons of the violins. As this finally died away, one was transported from the concert hall to some dim imagined field in a gray and cloud-rimmed English countryside; voice and violins became doubtful if not unreal horizon sounds; one seemed to hear not music but silence. . . . It was a moment of high art. No wonder the listeners fairly held their breaths, seemed almost audibly to sigh with their perception of this so native and peculiar beauty, before they burst forth in cheers for the unostentatious man on the platform, conducting like some friendly bear, who could perform this miracle for them, translating into tones what was

most individual and most dear to them in their
native land. . . . And the music, one may add,
took something from their friendly understanding; they gave as well as received. Neither at its
first performance (under the composer's direction) at a Norfolk Festival, nor later in Carnegie Hall, had it seemed so illuminated by those
who heard it, its essential character so empha-
sized by their response, as here in Queen's Hall,
speaking to its own people of their common
country.

There are naturally not many works so intensely
English as this reserved, almost monotonous *Pastoral Symphony* of Vaughan Williams: even his
own *London Symphony* is English city rather than
country—and the countryside is the essential England. That there were, nevertheless, plenty of fine
works to afford nucleating points for the six remaining programs of the 1930 British Composers'
Series we shall realize as we look through the list:
Elgar's two symphonies and his splendid *Enigma
Variations*; Bax's *Third Symphony*; William Wal-
lace's fascinatingly orchestrated, too seldom heard
symphonic poem *Villon*; to say nothing of lesser
works by Bantock, Berners, Bliss, Boughton, Delius, Goossens, Grainger, Holst, Lambert, Walton,
and others. How long will it be before we can

make so impressive a showing? According to
Vaughan Williams, possibly not more than a generation. Let us hope he may be right.

A point of subordinate importance, nevertheless
worth consideration, is the opportunity a scheme
of this kind gives for solo work with orchestral
accompaniment, a delightful department of music nowadays practically banned in New York.
Not only in the British programs but in the general ones much greater place is given to soloists
than is possible with us. In the four concerts in
the 1930 series on which these impressions are
based there appeared no less than four concertos
(Hindemith, organ; Elgar, violin; Tschaikowsky,
piano; Walton, viola), not to mention César
Franck's *Les Djinns,* with its prominent solo piano part. Of singing the same four concerts contained: two songs with orchestra by Strauss (how
many beautiful ones there are we never hear!); a
Benedictus by Dame Ethel Smyth; an aria of Doni-
zetti, tiresome and poorly sung; and an aria from
Elgar's *The Kingdom.* Roughly, five instrumental
and four vocal groups in four concerts. In the
same number of Carnegie Hall concerts what
would you probably get? Four guest-conductors,
probably—each, like the princesses in the fairy-
story, more remarkable than the others. But you

would be lucky if you got a single concerto; and as for arias, you would hardly dare confess an interest in them. And you could go to Carnegie Hall for a whole season without having a chance to hear such a work as Mahler's *First Symphony*—not an inspired nor even a highly significant work, but one that a music-lover with normal curiosity wants to hear, just as a normal lover of letters wants to dip into Beaumont and Fletcher once in a while as well as Shakspere and cannot accept any amount of Browning and Tennyson in lieu of the chance to find out for himself about, let us say, Walter Savage Landor or Thomas Love Peacock. In short, the Prom programs are not standardized (and stereotyped) by the box-office and the prejudices of the snobs. They fit happily into the living artistic experience of anyone who loves music better than musicians.

What are the lessons to be learned from the Promenade Concerts by American music-lovers? We cannot, of course, imitate literally in New York what works so well in London, not only because literal imitation is never creative, but more particularly because our conditions are fundamentally different. America is infinitely and bafflingly more complex than England. Thus for our composers there is no such clear, common,

universal emotion to be expressed as the sentiment of the English countryside, appealing more
or less to all Englishmen, that Vaughan Williams
has expressed in his *Pastoral Symphony*. The point
is not, as parrot-minded people are apt to think,
that American life is prosaic, commercial, and vulgar, and that there is nothing in it worthy of artistic expression. So far is this from being so that
the trouble with American life, to the artist, is
that there is too much in it clamoring for expression—too much, too widely scattered, addressing
too diverse groups, so that it can nowhere be uni-
fied. American life is vulgar and prosaic only to
the dull and the conventional, to those devoid of
fresh imagination; but to us all it is many-sided,
nowhere nucleated, and, as subject for art, cha-
otic. What is American, as a meadow in Kent or
Surrey is English? A New England hill pasture?
A southern plantation? A Colorado canyon? The
fierce turmoil of Chicago? The careless easy life
of New Orleans? The nervous glitter and clamor
of Broadway? A mesa in New Mexico or a mountain in California or Oregon? . . . All of these
things are American, but no one of them is exclusively American, and no one appeals to all
Americans. When Sir Henry Wood picked out
Arthur Shepherd's "Horizons" (*Four Western*

Pieces) as his one American novelty for 1930,[1] he made a good choice, for it is a characteristic, effective work by one of our most serious composers; but he might have found quite as much local color, though of a different shade, in Kelley's *New England Symphony,* or in Powell's *Old Virginia Overture,* or, for that matter, in any one of half a dozen pieces not geographical at all in their connotation, but none the less unmistakably American. We cannot afford, then, in theory any more than in practice, to narrow down American music to any one comparatively simple formula, such as can hold English, or French, or German, or Italian music without constricting them. This impossibility of narrow definition brings with it much bafflement and bewilderment of spirit for our creative minds, grave practical inconveniences and impediments,—but also unique opportunities and a stimulating challenge to self-reliance and to ceaseless experiment.

The cosmopolitan and miscellaneous character of our audiences involves us in as many quandaries as the diversity of our composers and of what they have to express. Inspiring as it may be to an Amer-

---

[1] Actually, because of non-arrival of the orchestral material, it could not be played in the 1930 season; the point here is merely that it was chosen.

ican composer to witness such complete community of feeling between artist and audience as that
testified by the reception at the Proms of Vaughan
Williams or Arnold Bax, it would be an idle day-
dream for him ever to expect such a reception in
America for any of his own music, or for that of
his fellows. How could any one piece of music
ever speak thus completely to any Carnegie Hall
audience, made up as it is of the races, groups,
cliques, the varying points of view and biases of
temperament of the whole world? Here again the
comparative simplicity of the give and take of artistic experience in a European country is un-
thinkable in our medley of peoples. All that we
can hope is that our geniuses may one day find
some way to take compensation for this very dis-
ability, to stamp with the unity without which art
cannot exist a diversity which offers possibilities
of such rich relationships, such exciting confron-
tations.

In the meantime, even if such higher syntheses
must await the geniuses alone capable of making
them, there are humbler, yet important, trends
of development in our American music to which
all sincerely music-loving and intelligently patriotic people may contribute. Everyone helps and
forwards our music who makes the effort to value

it for itself, as a sincere and unique expression, no matter how immediately successful or unsuccessful; everyone confuses and retards it who distracts attention to the manner of its performance, to the mere personalities of its creators and performers, or to its commercial returns. Here again, it must be admitted, our melting-pot public puts us at a disadvantage in comparison with more homogeneous European groups. A New York audience has almost no loyalty, public spirit, artistic piety. Made up as it is of Tom, Dick, and Harry, here today and gone tomorrow, it is a gaping, curious, cruel public, avid of sensation, eager for thrills and excitements, but too restless for deep emotion. In short, it is a public fated to idolize personalities and to ignore art, a public on which virtuosos and guest-conductors thrive as gross weeds thrive in a marsh. And it cares as little about the fascinating evolution of art itself as children at a menagerie care about the evolution of the animals they regard so idly.

How are we to combat this incubus of a miscellaneous, untrained, traditionless audience? How are we to create an atmosphere less negatively smothering or positively poisonous to the best potentialities of our music, an atmosphere in which it can grow normally? Shall we be obliged, in ways

envisaged in the preceding chapter, to give up
altogether the professional concert hall, as our
dramatic art has largely given up the commercial
theatre? Shall we have to fall back on amateur
groups such as school and college orchestras? It
is hard to believe this could ever satisfy us. Or,
possibly, shall we be able, understanding them,
gradually to reduce the virtuoso-worship and the
box-office servitude of our public concerts and
painfully to guide them to more disinterested and
creative attitudes? In this latter case we may find
help and hope in the example of the Promenade
Concerts. For they show us how healthily music
may develop when composers and public work
together in good understanding for its development, and when virtuosos, whether of an instrument, the voice, or the baton, are relegated to
their proper subordinate place and made the
happy servants rather than the vain and discon-
tented tyrants of musical art.

Chapter Eleven

SOME EMANCIPATIONS . . .

When Dr. Ralph Vaughan Williams, nowadays generally recognized as the leading figure of the flourishing contemporary school of English music, first visited America, in the spring of 1922, for the performance of his *Pastoral Symphony* at the Norfolk Festival, he prophesied that our American music would eventually emancipate itself, as the English had already done, from foreign domination. "You are about a generation behind us," he said. "Your present men are doing the preliminary educational work accomplished with us by Parry and Stanford. In twenty-five years you should have a school of native composers like ours today." "Between the years 1870 and 1915," writes another Englishman, Cecil Forsyth, "England has been able to assert her nationality in music. And this is a matter of the deepest interest to all Americans who love their country. Americ has yet to learn that only by the paths of nationalism can she scale the heights of internationalism." [1] And Sir Charles Stanford, himself one of the greatest of the English pioneers, has even explained why our emancipation has been so long delayed. Writing of the United States at the time of the Civil War, he says: "A nation of such recent growth and consisting of so many still unamalgamated elements, could not be expected to strike out a new and individual path. Nations have to grow old with a folk-music of centuries behind them before they express themselves in unmistakable terms of their own nationality. The ingredients have to be mixed and boiled before the dish is served. Upon this point Von Bülow and Dvořák were equally positive; both agreed in the prophecy that with patience the day of American music would come." [2]

In order to realize how close is the parallelism suggested by Vaughan Williams between our own conditions now and those of England a generation ago one has only to read some such realistic account of England's struggles as Fuller-Maitland's *English Music in the Nineteenth Century*, published

---

[1] "The English Musical Renaissance," in *The Art of Music*, Volume III, Chapter xiii.

[2] "Music and the War," in *Interludes*, by Charles V. Stanford (London, 1922).

in 1902. At that time the present leaders were just beginning to be heard of: "R. Vaughan Williams" is mentioned as the composer of an orchestral elegy, and as having strong individuality; and we read that "G. von Holst is certain to go far." (The "von" was dropped after the war). The analogies with our own situation are laughably exact. If London, like New York today, was overrun by foreign musicians, we may comfort ourselves that the author saw in this condition one of the causes of the renaissance, since "it prepared the soil in which the seed of genius, once sown, could flourish rapidly." The sowing, however, was proceeding with all the difficulties we know so dishearteningly. Longing was voiced for a time when "Mr." Henry J. Wood (since knighted, in large measure for his services to English music) should adopt "a rather more patriotic policy in regard to the choice of music, giving due prominence to the noble English works which lie awaiting performance, rather than to every production, good or bad, of the new Russian school." Add Italian to Russian, and how like Carnegie Hall it sounds! And no American composer will read without qualms that "It is the habit of giving (often with great reluctance) single performances of English works, and then imagining that such performances are of themselves an encouragement to

146

native art, that has done more than almost anything else to retard the progress of our national
music." Yet there was already a group of leaders—
Mackenzie, Parry, Goring Thomas, Cowen, Stanford—who, as the author insists, "although they are
musicians, are intelligent, cultivated people at the
same time." To these leaders, so similar in type to
ours now, he attributes the conscious co-operation
which initiated the actual renaissance, early in the
eighties. Like ours, these leaders were usually dis-
missed as "academic" by the press, whose skill is
slyly stated to have been about equal to discovering
that they were connected with the universities.
"These leaders have shown real inspiration," asserts Fuller-Maitland; "their music comes mainly
from the heart, not merely from the head. The
truth is that the word 'academic,' as used by these
journalists, may best be defined as an epithet ap-
plied to those who understand their work by those
who do not."

Everywhere music was being hampered by the
conventionality and timidity of such opinions,
both in the critics and in the public; and above all
by their servile idolatry of foreign prestige: it was
the overwhelming incubus of the vogue of Handel
and Mendelssohn, as the author shows in detail, that
for generations stifled all English originality. How

many thousands of dull oratorios have been perpetrated in England on the model of *The Messiah*? How many composers have repudiated their personalities in order to become, like Sterndale Bennett, tamer English replicas of the already tame Mendelssohn? Like the similar subservience to foreign fashion that now weighs upon us, of which we have only recently become conscious and which we still find ourselves rather helpless to combat, this servility had the unreasonableness, the automatic, mechanical, fatal quality of all fashions, and like all fashions was maintained chiefly by the wealthier and more socially powerful classes. As with us, the simpler people who loved their own environment and could appreciate its beauty were overborne by the snobs and sophisticates. So it has always been. All significant emancipations have been revolts against the tyranny of fashion by people in love with local, homely, simple, and unaffected beauty.

Of the two most musical of nations, Italy and Germany, only the former, by its domination of all Europe, escaped the necessity of self-assertion. Germany had to emancipate itself from Italian influence, in the rejection of Italianized opera by Mozart and Weber, continued later, on a more formidable scale, by Wagner. In the Russian national-

istic movement of the early nineteenth century, led
by Glinka and later by Balakireff, there was a re-
pudiation of both Italian and German models. The
French, after the Franco-Prussian War, in the
movement so interestingly described as *"Le renou-
veau"* in Romain Rolland's *Musiciens d'aujour-
d'hui,* freed themselves not only from Italianism,
but from Wagnerism, from certain heavy, anti-
Gallic features of German symphonic music from
Haydn to Brahms, and from the megalomania of
Mahler and Strauss. As for ourselves, the foreign
domination is so complete and so overwhelming,
as a glance at the programs of the Philharmonic–
Symphony Society or the Metropolitan Opera will
show, that the only pertinent question so far seems
to be: Have we any music of our own at all?

If we ask, however, as a preliminary to answering
it, what "music of their own" the other nations
turned to in their emancipations, the answer is not
a simple one. Many people will reply dogmatically:
"Folk-song. There is no other basis for a national
music." No doubt it is true that in all significant
emancipations folk-song has played an important
part. The folk-element in Weber's operas, and even
in Wagner's *Die Meistersinger,* is unmistakable.
The Russian *"Kutschka,"* or "Invincible Band,"
led by Balakireff, founded their theory and practice

frankly on folk-so   A number of them edited
collections of the   tive songs; César Cui wrote
fanatically in defense of them; Borodin used them
in his symphonies; Rimsky-Korsakoff and Moussorgsky incorporated them in their operas. . . .
The English renaissance confessedly owes much to
Cecil Sharp's tireless collecting; and more skilful
musicians than he, such as Grainger, Butterworth,
and above all Vaughan Williams, have both tran-
scribed and idealized the popular songs in works
for the stage and for the concert hall. Even in
France, where aristocratic elegance counts for so
much in all the arts, the people have made their
contributions, and Rolland devotes an impressive
section of his essay to *"La musique et le peuple."*

Now if we are going to take the folk-song enthusiasts literally it may as well be admitted at
once that the chances for an American emancipation are poor. We have here, it cannot be denied,
no compact and well-defined body of music like
those to which nationalists in Germany, Russia,
France, and England have successively and so successfully turned. It is not that we have no folk-
songs; we suffer rather from an embarrassment of
riches, from bewilderment as to which of our
many bodies of native song really represent and
express our highly composite national individual-

ity. The music of the Indian aborigines is narrow, monotonous, musically uninteresting. Negro music, however beautiful and expressive, is emotionally childlike, not to say primitive. Beautiful are the Anglo-Saxon tunes of the Eastern mountains; so are the Creole tunes of the South, the cow-boy songs of the West; but which of them are "American," and in what sense? Any attempt to found either the theory or the practice of our music on folk-songs seems, for so racially, nationally, and culturally miscellaneous a people as we are, foredoomed to failure.[1]

It is rather solacing, therefore, to reflect that even for simpler national units like Russia, France, or England, the folk-song theory, taken fanatically, is too sweeping, is over-literal and unimaginative in spirit, and is accordingly discounted or qualified by the shrewder critics. Of English nationalism in the narrower sense, for instance, Ernest Newman had the courage to say, even in its heyday just after the war: "The nationalists isolate a certain genre of expression—the folk-song of generations ago—and tell us that only by absorbing this genre into his tissues can an English composer hope to be English. That, I claim, is a monstrous fallacy.

---

[1] For further discussion of these vexing problems, see the author's *The Dilemma of American Music.*

. . . If he feels deeply and sincerely about life, and can find beautiful and convincing expression for what he and the rest of us living people feel, he will make great English art even though he may never have heard a folk-song and never have seen an agricultural labourer." It is enlightening to compare this with an article by C. W. Orr in the *Musical Times* for January, 1931, on "Elgar and the Public." After showing that Elgar's earlier fame with his own countrymen was based, not on understanding, but on the foreign prestige reflected upon him by the praise of Richter and Strauss, that the first performance of his *Falstaff* was largely to empty benches, and that during the time after the war "when folk-tunes became all the rage, and young composers diligently flattened their sevenths and modalised their tunes" he was still neglected, the author insists that Elgar had none the less "contrived to write music as 'English' as any of the newer generation without the factitious aid of folk-song and its inevitable accompanying mannerisms." He attributes his recent overwhelming successes in England to his "showing himself like some 'sea-shouldering whale' among the little dolphins and porpoises who have floundered uncomfortably in his immense wake," and to the gratitude of the public for his music, "coming

like a health-giving tonic, which has been thank-
fully swallowed by audiences sick of the acidities
of too many Bright Young People. . . . It is becoming more and more evident," concludes the
article, "that he, who has never worried about
'nationalism,' is the most *national* of all our composers. His music could have been written only by
an Englishman. Many of his movements might be
labelled *Allegro Democraticamente,* so redolent
are they of all that is most essentially English—
jovial humour and unaffected sincerity."

Here the emphasis is shifted from the narrower
sense of nationalism as depending on the use of a
local idiom to a larger and freer sense, carrying
the idea of truth to a particular psychological type
or temperament. Elgar is English temperamentally
(and of course unconsciously) in that he reacts to
life with a certain peculiarly English emotional
attitude. For this deeper view idiom is of secondary
importance. Elgar's idiom, as a matter of fact, contains little modal melody or harmony, or anything
suggesting folk-music save perhaps sometimes
traces of the rhythms of English dance. Harmoni-
cally it is rather German, so that a harmonic analysis would reveal much the same material we
find in Brahms or Wagner. Yet no one who has
studied him can doubt that in his best music he

uses his material in his own way. His use of inter-
locked seventh chords, for example, is highly individual and gives to such a bit as the theme of the
Enigma Variations an aspect eminently personal.
His temperament writes its signature, so to speak,
on all his best work, in a sort of rugged, homely
sincerity, an earnestness never hysterical or over-
subjective, reticent and self-respecting, yet vibrant
and intense, that we recognize as indescribably
but unmistakably English. Similarly, even in a
composer so committed to folk-song as Vaughan
Williams we find pieces like the *Pastoral Symphony,* from which, despite the unobtrusiveness or
even the absence of the folk-element, there yet
breathes a spirit poignantly suggestive of England,
of her green hedgerows and gray skies, of the undemonstrative friendliness of her people.

The thought that national individuality may be
more temperamental than idiomatic helps us,
again, to understand the controversies that raged
about and between Tschaikowsky and the Russian
"Invincible Band." The nationalists, led by Balakireff, propagated in the press by César Cui, and
touching greatness in the person of Moussorgsky,
were passionately committed to the folk-song
dogma and gave Tschaikowsky many hard digs because he was not. He, for his part, while remaining

friendly to them, writing some of his own works on programs suggested by Balakireff and Stassoff, and even incorporating Little Russian folk-themes in his *Second Symphony*, never took their fanaticisms seriously and, as time went on, gradually detached himself from narrow nationalism. Thus it comes about that his most characteristic works—the *Fifth* and *Sixth* symphonies, the *Piano Concerto, Romeo and Juliet*—not only wear no folk-costumes, but are stylistically just about as Germano-cosmopolitan in idiom as Elgar. Yet how intensely Russian they are! Their Russianism, however, is a matter not of melodic or harmonic texture but of temperament (like Elgar's English quality, though at the opposite pole): it is in their passionate subjectivity of mood (as against Elgar's reticence), in their profound gloom and their frenzied climaxes of uncontrolled feeling that they are Russian; and therein they are far more significantly Russian, or rather, since race is wider and deeper than nation, more significantly Slavic, than many unexceptionably "nationalistic" works whose every cadence makes that descent from the fourth to the first step of the scale which hall-marks it "Russian." The Bright Young People, no doubt, still turn up their noses at Tschaikowsky, quite as they do at Elgar: they find both "banal." But the world at large has accepted Tschaikowsky as more deeply and essentially Russian than any of the nationalists save Moussorgsky, just as it seems to be about to place Elgar beside Vaughan Williams as the most winningly English of living composers.

In France the case of Vincent d'Indy is instructive. Today, near the end of his long life packed with significant and beautiful work, he is still appreciated only by the few. The followers of current fashions, joined by the faddists, who in France are less apt to be nationalists than sophisticates, eclectics, and pseudo-intellectuals, cry him down; and sounder opinion has not as yet consciously reacted against them. Vincent d'Indy is, however, the most profoundly French of living composers. And his French quality, like Elgar's English and Tschaikowsky's Russian, is rather in temperament than in texture, more of the spirt than of the letter. He did, to be sure, in his early *Symphony on a Mountain Theme,* use the melodies of his beloved Cévennes country; the precise and evenly accented syllables of French song sound through many of his most characteristic themes in all his works; there is hardly one of his scherzos that does not recall the general mode of utterance of, say, *Sur le pont d'Avignon.* But all this is superficial beside the deeply Gallic love of clearness, dislike of ex-aggeration, pure, austere, and intense feeling, that live in all his greater works. This austerity, this reticent passion of D'Indy, which those who do not understand him describe as "cerebral," is both his most personal and his most national trait. The strain it has inspired, in *Istar,* in *A Summer Day on the Mountain,* in the *Quartet in E major,* is one of the profoundest and sweetest strains that has ever come out of France. Few hear it today, but its tender beauty will not always fall on deaf or in-different ears.

Chapter Twelve

. . . AND A MORAL

These examples and considerations seem to offer us some encouragement in our hope of achieving our own individuality despite the confused state of musical idiom in our country. Vital nationalism, they suggest, depends less on distinctive idioms, even for those nations that possess them, than on distinctive temperamental attitudes toward life, and on loyalty to local experience, displacing servility to foreign points of view, and prompting in its place a simple sincerity of expression. In their light we realize that in order to achieve our own individuality it is less necessary for us to isolate a characteristic body of folk-song than to analyze our characteristic attitudes or temperamental tendencies in ourselves, become clearly conscious of them, and gradually, overcoming our sense of inferiority to nations more advanced in art, take our stand unflinchingly upon them.

Such a characteristic American attitude, for instance, to take first a fairly simple and clear case,

is the reserve, the dislike of ostentation, the repressed but strong emotion masked by dry humor,
that belong to our New England type, as we have
seen it in Elgar to belong to the prevailing type
in the older England. This Anglo-Saxon element in our heterogeneous national character,
however quantitatively in the minority nowadays,
is qualitatively of crucial significance in determin-
ing what we call the American temper. The name
popularly symbolizing it—the word "Yankee"—is
often extended from New England to cover the
whole country; and that other and most far-
reaching of all our popular symbols—Uncle Sam—
is only a universalized and glorified Yankee. In
our literature the type is immortally enshrined in
the work of Emerson and Thoreau and, in our own
day, of Robinson and Frost. We hear it often in
the music of Chadwick, sometimes in MacDowell
and in Hill (a sort of tender reticence), in Kelley's
New England Symphony, and in Powell's overture *In Old Virginia* (for it belongs to the old South
as well as to New England). The essence of it is
a kind of moderation—not negative, as those who
do not understand it imagine, but strongly positive;
the moderation that, as Chesterton says, is "not a
compromise, but a passion, the passion of great
judges"; a moderation, in Tennyson's fine phrase:

Turning to scorn with lips divine
The falsehood of extremes.

Why an attitude thus based on moderation
should have received so far such slight and sporadic
expression in our music, instead of infusing it with
a pervasive and dominating individuality, is not
hard to understand when we reflect that the particular type of foreign prestige to which we have
most completely capitulated is precisely that Jewish
type which, if not exactly based on the "falsehood
of extremes," at least tolerates, perhaps even en-
joys, extremes, as a soberer music cannot. The Jew
and the Yankee stand, in human temperament,
at polar points; where one thrives, the other is
bound to languish. And our whole contemporary
æsthetic attitude toward instrumental music, especially in New York, is dominated by Jewish tastes
and standards, with their Oriental extravagance,
their sensuous brilliancy and intellectual facility
and superficiality, their general tendency to ex-
aggeration and disproportion. "The insidiousness
of the Jewish menace to our artistic integrity,"
wrote the present writer more than ten years ago,[1]
when the domination was far less complete than it

[1] "Is American Music Growing Up? Our Emancipation from Alien
Influences," in *Arts and Decoration*, November, 1920.

has since become, "is due to the speciousness, the superficial charm and persuasiveness of Hebrew art, its violently juxtaposed extremes of passion, its poignant eroticism and pessimism. . . . For how shall a public accustomed by prevailing fashion to the exaggeration, the constant running to extremes, of eastern expression, divine the poignant beauty of Anglo-Saxon sobriety and restraint? How shall it pierce the Anglo-Saxon reticence, the fine reserve so polar to the garrulous self-confession, the almost indecent stripping of the soul, it witnesses in every concert hall and opera house? How shall it value as it deserves the balance, the sense of proportion, which is the finest of Anglo-Saxon qualities, and to which, like the sense of humor to which it is akin (since both depend upon the sense of congruity or incongruity), nothing is more alien than the Oriental abandonment to excess? Our public taste is in danger of being permanently debauched, made lastingly insensitive to qualities most subtly and quintessentially our own, by the intoxication of what is, after all, an alien art."

It was several years after these warnings had been written that Ernest Bloch, long the chief minister of that intoxication to our public, capped his dealings with us by the grim jest of presenting to us a long, brilliant, megalomaniac, and thoroughly

Jewish symphony—entitled *America*. (In calling attention to this irony, it is hardly necessary to state that no "anti-Jewish propaganda" is intended. All propaganda is apt to be either indifferent or positively injurious to art. Besides, no judgment on the intrinsic value of the Jewish element in American art in general, or of Mr. Bloch's music in particular, is here undertaken. All that is being pointed out is that our own subservience to fashion allows one type of art to make us deaf to the possibilities of another that is more peculiarly our own.)

If we look for idiosyncrasies more widespread among us than the ancestral Anglo-Saxon seriousness, our attention may fall on what has been called "American hustle"—a group of qualities induced or encouraged by our present business and industrial life, such as haste, practical "efficiency," good humor of a superficial sort, inventiveness, an extravert preference of action to thought—in short, all that is suggested by such popular slogans as "Step lively" and "Keep smiling." Its natural musical expression is found, of course, in jazz; and for a long time now certain critics have been persistently telling us that jazz is in fact the one distinctive American music, and that by cultivating it sedulously we shall find our musical "place in the sun" among the nations. In jazz, moreover, suppression of native qualities by imported standards seems not to be in operation. On the contrary, jazz has been distinctly "taken up" by some of the more advanced European groups, for whom America has thus become a source of musical importations as well as the ever profitable market for exports. If jazz, as one of its panegyrists claims, expresses "the jerk and rattle" of the American city, "its restless bustle and motion, its multitude of unrelated details, and its underlying progress toward a vague somewhere" [1] and if this expression of the more trivial side of American life meets with no such opposition from fashion as confronts that of more serious aspects, the question inevitably arises whether we should not find here a hopeful lead for American music. In spite of these apparently promising features, however, the answer given by the more discerning critics from the first, and recently with increasing inescapability by experience itself, has turned out to be a negative one, for reasons that throw some light on our whole problem.

First of all, jazz is not, like the varied types of European folk-song to which it is often misleadingly

---

[1] Hiram K. Moderwell, in the *New Republic,* October 16, 1915.

compared, a spontaneous artistic activity of our people; it is a commercial product, like so many others "put over" upon the people. It does not grow up in simple minds, voicing their feelings; it is manufactured by calculating ones, seeking profit. In a word, it is not an expression at all; it is an exploitation. Consequently, instinctively felt by all sensitive minds to be artificial, it leaves them cold; it has no persuasiveness, no magic, no psychological truth.

In the second place, even if jazz were true, its truth would be to a pathological state in us, not to the mental health on which alone a valid art can be reared. For it reflects, not our health, vitality, and hope, but our restlessness, our fatigue, and our despair. It is a symptom of a sick moment in the progress of the human soul: the moment of industrial turmoil, fever, and distress that we can but hope to survive, not to perpetuate. To its tense, false gayety the hearing ear responds never with the joy that comes only in relaxation, but with a sense of depression that may be tinged with tragedy. Even its most distinguished exploiters seem to recognize its hysterical character. Ernest Schelling's *A Victory Ball* is built on a program of post-war disillusion. Mr. Carpenter's *Skyscrapers* is said to represent "the hurry and din of American life

. . . its violent alternations of work and play." Despite its kinship with an undeniable if superficial side of our character, and in spite of its acceptability to Europeans in search rather of new sensations than of living art, the bankruptcy of jazz as a source of serious music is becoming daily more evident.[1]

Yet surely there is something in this liveliness of ours, this brisk good cheer, this kindly if superficial cordiality, that gives significance and distinctiveness to our national character. Perhaps, if we could but detach it from the morbid excitement of jazz, product of industrial cities poisoned with nervous fatigue, it might afford a valid ingredient in our art. One hears such a quality, tranquilized and balanced, as it were, by open air and wide spaces, without losing any of its energy, in much of Grainger and Powell and in such a real American folksong as David Guion's *Turkey in the Straw*. Such animation is native to us, as that in the finales of Haydn's symphonies was native to his Croatian people. It is like the liveliness of children, innocent and gay. Genuinely American is this childlike innocence, since we are in our fundamental mentality childlike or even childish, not to say infantile.

---

[1] For more detailed discussions, see the present writer's chapter on "Music in America," in *Contemporary Composers*, and "The Jazz Invasion," in the symposium *Behold America*.

And this brings us to a final trait of ours, perhaps potentially the most American of all, though for the present suffering the severest repression: our sentiment. There can be no doubt that sentiment, often of the naïvest, most unself-conscious kind, existing in a separate compartment from our humor and untouched by it, is a deep ingredient of our character. Not only the American of nineteenth-century fiction, but the American of twentieth-century fact, is naïve in a way and to a degree often surprising to Europeans; his emotions, wonders, vanities, ideals, hopes, are those of a child, not yet made realist by bitter experience. Our most characteristic men of letters both depict these traits and illustrate them in their own persons; think of the trusting optimism of Emerson, the boyish swagger of Bret Harte and Mark Twain, the childish sentimentality of James Whitcomb Riley and Ella Wheeler Wilcox, the o'erleaping romanticism, unchecked by sober fact, of Walt Whitman. Musically, too, childlike sentiment forms a definite line in our tradition: we hear it in the untutored songs of Stephen Foster, in the sentiment often verging on sentimentality of Nevin, in the thoroughgoing unashamed romanticism of MacDowell, often felt for this very quality to be our most characteristic composer. We find it today, in varying shades and degrees, in the music of Hadley, Hanson, Hill, Mason, Powell, and Deems Taylor.

Now it is an undeniable fact, of the most far-reaching import to our future growth, that precisely this childlike sentiment, perhaps our deepest quality, surely one of our most characteristic, is the one most irreconcilably antipathetic of all to the qualities of European music that at present set the vogue all over the world, and consequently the one most relentlessly repressed by them. A childlike people, in both the good and the bad senses of the word, musically undeveloped but promising, we find ourselves paralyzed on the very threshold of musical experience by the disillusionment, the cynicism, the blasé striving after novelty, of a Europe old and in some ways effete. The ruling fashion among the sophisticates today is neo-classicism, a dry, hard æsthetic which derides sentiment, repudiates romance, and almost measures the success of a piece of music by the absence of all expression from it. And the pity is that in a complete capitulation to these foreign models our young composers have almost to a man abjured their youth, personal and national. They are like conscientious and aspiring school drunkards and college roués, as pathetic as they are absurd. One

167

hardly knows whether to laugh or cry when one
hears young Bostonians striving to outdo Schönberg in sterile, ugly counterpoint, young New
Yorkers vying with Stravinsky in brittle pseudo-
classicism, young Californians trying to be more
starkly primitive than Prokofieff!

If instead they would only, after learning all the
technique the European sophisticates have to teach
them, throw their æsthetic into the Atlantic Ocean
and start out afresh for themselves, in their own
childish romantic way, on what Walt Whitman
used to call "these shores"! If they would only dis-
cover that the game of following the fashions is
stupid, that the only satisfaction is in writing music
they themselves enjoy. From time to time it is re-
freshing to read of someone who has thus had the
courage to strike out for himself. Dr. Howard Hanson did it when he actually entitled his second
symphony *Romantic*. "As the sub-title implies,"
he explained, "it represents for me a definite em-
bracing of the romantic phase. Though there is
no story connected with this symphony, it was conceived as an escape from the rather bitter type
of modern musical realism which occupies so large
a place in contemporary thought. My aim has been
to create a work young in spirit, romantic in temperament and simple and direct in expression."

"We are a very different people from the French," says Douglas Moore in describing his first symphony, "and I cannot believe that the fashions decreed by such elegant couturiers as the Parisian Stravinsky or Ravel, successful as they are in permitting a post-war Europe to express herself, are likely to be appropriate or becoming to us. There are few of our endeavors in which we excel by pure cerebration. The best of what we accomplish is usually achieved by dint of high spirits, soft-heartedness, and a great deal of superfluous energy."

It is inspiring to hear the young men talking like that. One dares to hope that at last we are getting ready to outgrow our unmanly awe of Europe, preparing to look hopefully about us at our own life, and, interpreting it as it strikes our naïve, unspoiled sentiment, make some music of our own.

CHAPTER THIRTEEN

AN ÆSTHETIC FOR AMERICA

So far we have been considering, with a necessary limitation of view, the immediate conditions and problems of musical development as they press upon us here in America. It is now time to take a wider view, to seek to universalize our conclusions, to see whether in fact what is good for America is not also good for the whole world. We have been pleading for a courageous belief in naïve sentiment and sincere feeling, in the teeth of all fashionable sophistications, as necessary to the salvation of music in our country. Is it anything else that the whole world needs today? What are the most essential qualities of great music, always and everywhere? In what measure are they present or absent in the music of today, at home and abroad? What reasonable hope may we have of their increase, here or elsewhere, in the music of tomorrow?

To begin with, then, music is of all the arts proverbially the most emotional. In comparison with literature, for instance, it compensates for an inferior power in dealing with specific detail by a deeper eloquence in the presentation of fundamental moods and attitudes. Its penetration to the profoundest levels of our consciousness is akin to that of philosophy; but it expresses emotionally, as Schopenhauer recognized more fully than most philosophers, what philosophy only formulates intellectually. In so far, then, as our contemporary music has turned a cold shoulder upon emotion, it has repudiated its most essential quality and foregone its supreme advantage.

For the adoption of this curious attitude there are a number of causes. Aside from general social influences like the puritan's distrust of emotion and the "practical" man's contempt for beauty, the almost superstitious reverence of the modern mind for science has made it skeptical of all values not expressible in rigorously intellectual terms. Science creates the pervasive mental atmosphere of our time, an atmosphere in which, at least so long as science maintained its nineteenth-century materialism, emotional values could not breathe. To this pervasive atmosphere the war added a catastrophic event which through its disappointment of fallacious enthusiasms set up a reaction of cynicism, made us suspicious of all sentiment, and launched the cult of anti-romanticism. The result was the ultra-modernist attitude toward emotion conveniently summed up in the story of Stravinsky's thanking Josef Hofmann for playing a work of his absolutely to perfection—exactly as he wanted it—completely without expression.

Partly effect, partly in turn cause, of this ban on emotion is the extraordinary development among our modern sophisticates of the purely intellectual, or pseudo-intellectual, explanation of music, replacing the emotional experience of it; music, it has been said, used to be made to be enjoyed, but is now made to be discussed. Indifferent or even averse to such discussion have always been the truly creative minds, in which the path from emotion to expression is direct and the creative act naïve and unselfconscious. "X," wrote Brahms to a friend, "has the frightful habit of always philosophizing about music and musicians, and Wagner in particular gives him great scope in this respect. You know how I hate to analyze musicians and their tendencies." [1] Verdi's reply to a young man who tried to engage him in a discussion of the ethics of art and other imposing topics was: "What does it matter? Work." [2] And a discerning French critic has said: *"Il faut*

---

[1] Letters of Clara Schumann and Johannes Brahms, page 13.
[2] *Masters in Music,* Verdi number, page 5.

172

écouter à la musique comme un brute"—"One must listen to music like an innocent." [1]

But in place of this innocence, this fecund naïveté, we find in ultra-modernism a sterile sophistication, a restless itch for formulas. Music can no longer be just music; it must be atonal, or polytonal, or polyrhythmic, or primitive, or impressionistic, or symbolistic. It is even the fashion now to make it to specifications—as, for example, these, taken from an actual program of the New School of Social Research:

"The first movement opens with a quietly announced theme developed canonically; an auxiliary theme consists of repeated tones which rise by half-steps with each measure. . . .

"The third movement has a longer melodic line made of only two intervals, but placed in various ways one after the other. Rhythmical augmentation and diminution is present. . . ." etc., etc.

Indeed, your genuine modernist composer cannot write three notes without equipping them with three paragraphs of explanatory comment. Comparing sadly the voluminousness of his "blurb" with the exiguity of his musical ideas, we recall the man who said that most modern literature seemed

---

[1] M. Léon Vallas, quoted by Harold Bauer in "A Plea for the Amateur," *Musical America,* February 10, 1931.

to be "either erotic, neurotic, or Tommyrotic."

Our hope for the future of music must rest on the perception that all this splutter of talk is superficial and highly transitory, that the opposing cliques of ultra-modernists drown and cancel each other out, and that far deeper and more permanent forces are silently working to reinstate the emotion they contemn. Not the least of these forces today is science itself. Twentieth-century science has pretty completely sloughed off the superficial nineteenth-century materialism and, at the same time that it has substituted energy for matter, has grown in all its concepts more humanistic and begins to pay an unwonted respect to spiritual values. One cannot read far in Eddington, Millikan, or Whitehead without feeling the complete change of attitude; Overstreet, in his recent *The Enduring Quest,* specifically discusses the significance of art to science; this significance is well summarized in the following passage from J. W. N. Sullivan's *Aspects of Science:*

"Mathematics is of profound significance not because it exhibits principles that we obey, but because it exhibits principles that we impose. It shows us the laws of our own being and the necessary conditions of experience. And is it not true that the other arts do something similar in those regions of

174

experience which are not of the intellect alone? May it not be that the meaning Beethoven declared his music to possess is that, although man seems to live in an alien universe, yet it is true of the whole of experience as well as of that part of it which is the subject of science that what man finds is what he has created, and that the spirit of man is indeed free, eternally subject only to its own decrees?" [1]

And here is what a biologist—Julian Huxley—has to say of the supreme importance of art: "There are those to whom Truth is the final goddess. . . . But there can be a bondage to truth, and until we are free there is no perfection. The escape of thought from the imperfections of the actual into a thought-organized ideal is Art; its projection, dragging present action with it into a more perfect future, is true religion. . . . Only when we combine our search for verifiable truth with these utmost aspirations do we become perfect men. That is why the 'mere' scientist is not great; that is why art or literature without the passion for truth is trivial and empty. The true man would be he who was always combining, in every activity, this whole hierarchy of mutually reinforcing modes of mind." [2]

---

[1] J. W. N. Sullivan: *Aspects of Science, Second Series*, page 95.
[2] Julian Huxley: *Essays in Popular Science*, page 189.

175

Even today the "true men" of music, our really great composers, are thus subordinating the "mere science" of the modernists to that "passion for truth" which in music takes the fundamental form of emotional attitudes. While Strauss, for instance, has taken at times plenty of the modernist's interest in mere idiom, as we see in his experiments in *Elektra* and *Salome,* it is by his broadly human interpretations, in *Till Eulenspiegel* and in lighter vein in *Der Rosenkavalier,* that we remember him, and that he will live. Similarly, in contemporary France Vincent d'Indy may be for the moment neglected by a generation charmed by the enticing sonorities of Debussy and Ravel or amused by the impish pranks of the "Six"; but, as he has himself said: *"Il n'est que le cœur pour engendrer de la beauté";* and a world that in the long run loves beauty will return to him. In Italy Malipiero and Casella devise the startling or piquant formulas that sound interesting in newspaper reports and dinner conversations, Respighi caters incomparably for those addicted to a rich orchestral diet, but Pizzetti will last better than any of them because he is more deeply emotional and more inclusively human. In the same way, in England the unstriking but profoundly individual Elgar and Vaughan Williams wear better than the superficially cleverer

Holst, Holbrooke, Berners, Bliss, and others. As time goes on, as the cheap cynicism of ultra-modern sophistication begins to pall upon us, and as modern science with its increasingly human emphasis continues to confirm our instinctive values, it is to be hoped that more and more composers will turn to this sounder ideal of emotional expression.

Along with depth of emotion, let us now note further, always go richness and definiteness of individuality. For example, Strauss, D'Indy, Pizzetti, Elgar, and Vaughan Williams are not only profounder in emotional expression than their lesser fellows, but more different from each other, more individually distinct and original. And on this sort of individuality we rightly insist as a quality of all the greatest music. Yet we are at present allowing much of the potential individuality of our young composers to be inhibited and defeated by wrong notions of what true individuality is; and if we really wish our future composers to be fruitfully individual, we might make them at least the modest contribution of a little clear thinking on the subject.

The first requisite of a rich individuality is a rich tradition: without the nourishment that he can draw only from his great fellows of the past, the artist cannot form his values, his standards of taste, his sense of proportion—in short, all that is deepest and most essential in his artistic personality. True as this is of all the arts, it is peculiarly true of music, the very materials of which do not exist in the external world, as do those of literature, painting, and sculpture, and can therefore be drawn only from music itself. Hence all great musicians depend in their early stages very strictly upon their forerunners: early Beethoven is Haydn and Mozart; early Wagner is Weber and Meyerbeer; even early Stravinsky is Rimsky-Korsakoff. Moreover, the richer the individuality, the more varied are its derivations and the longer it takes to mature. César Franck, whose music becomes fully his own only when he is about sixty, and all of whose masterpieces belong to his last decade, derives from the polyphony of Bach, the free-variation principle of late Beethoven, and the chromaticism of Wagner, to mention only the most obvious elements. The general rule seems to be: the more powerful the eventually emergent individuality, the wider its traditional sources, the more imitative its early works, and the longer delayed its maturity. One recalls John Fiske's theory that the superiority of man to other animals is conditioned by the greater length of his period of helpless infancy.

Of all the ill effects of our present snobbish so-

phistication, therefore, one of the worst is its disposition to allow the young composer no period
of artistic infancy at all. If he imitates anything
richer than the current fashions, it calls him "unoriginal"; if he shows traces of that loving study of
his predecessors which is instinctive with all truly
artistic natures, it brands him as "academic"; it re-
serves its praises for those who are what it calls
"original" (that is to say, eccentric) at twenty, and
who will therefore be played out and forgotten at
thirty. (How surprisingly many old young men
ultra-modernism produces, contrasting oddly with
the young old men of the richer tradition, preserved
by their naïveté: Haydn, Verdi, Franck, Brahms!)
The critics of our daily press bear a heavy responsi-
bility here. They are always urging originality on
the young, giving them no time to develop the kind
of originality that has depth and value. The New
York *Times* not long ago blamed a piano concerto
by one of our younger men for being "principally
Tschaikowsky and Rachmaninoff in style," and ad-
vised the composer to "wait until a vital idea had
evolved before attempting to build up with straw a
three-movement concerto." It did not seem to oc-
cur to the *Times* that Tchaikowsky and Rachmaninoff may be among the best models for a young
man of twenty-seven who is trying to find himself,

or that one of the indispensable means for getting ideas is to study, think, and write. Almost at random one picks up another copy of the same paper and reads: "Elgar's music [*Introduction and Allegro,* for strings, played by Toscanini] has nothing of a revolutionary character about it, but it is very well made. . . ." Well, why in heaven's name *should* it have "anything of a revolutionary character" about it? Is not true art evolutionary rather than revolutionary? Is not Elgar, with his peculiarly English reticence and detachment, his curiously low-keyed yet unmistakable nobility of feeling, one of the most individual musicians in the world today? "The Creator," says Yeats, "yawns in earthquake and thunder and other popular displays, but toils in rounding the delicate spiral of a shell." Our journalists, however, continue to prefer earthquake and thunder, which doubtless make better "copy" than loving workmanship, and to offer premiums to young composers for superficial eccentricity.

Probably the only ultimate cure for these fashionable fallacies is the good sense and idealism of the individual composer, who will oppose himself to them in the future as he has always done in the past, simply from his instinctive sense of what he needs for his own inner nourishment. Certainly individual discernment and courage seem the only things that can help him in the final stage of the achievement of individuality, the stage of selection from the rich materials opened up to him by tradition. Here again he will be wise to be on his guard against the miscellaneity of interest of the pure intellectual, the talker in drawing-rooms. The creative artist should have no illusions of his own comprehensiveness or impartiality. These are admirable qualities, but they are for the critic, not for the creator, whose deepest nature condemns him to a passionate partiality. His whole motivation is emotional, not intellectual. Both he and the critic require wide and deep study, but while the critic uses it impersonally, to arrive at balanced judicial conclusions, the artist uses it personally, to fecundate his own genius. For this he has to have the courage of his convictions, even of his prejudices, to be highly selective, to take what he can use, to reject what, however excellent for others, is not for him. In a sophisticated age he has to dare to be naïve. In brief, he must read and reread Emerson's *Self-Reliance,* take it to heart and try to live it.

In the measure that he can do that, his individuality will become not only wide and rich through tradition, but profound and original through personal conviction. And it is only

through the co-operative labors of many such individuals, supported by a similarly intelligent society,
that we can hope to see our music free itself from
the inhibitions with which ultra-modernism has
paralyzed it (as materialism paralyzed nineteenth-
century science), and gradually exchange its present
sophistication, anæmia, and fashionable monotony
for naïveté, vigor richly nourished by tradition, and
potent individuality.

CHAPTER FOURTEEN

WHAT SHALL WE DO
ABOUT IT?

When we Americans ask ourselves what practical
steps to take about anything, our reply is apt to
shape itself in terms of endowment or of organization rather than of personal effort. The results of
individual effort are too slow and too intangible to
satisfy our impatience; it is quicker to give money
or to appoint a committee or found a society. In
matters of art, however, what can be done by endowing or organizing seems to be relatively slight
and unimportant; art seems to be almost necessarily personal in initiative, and our habitual approach seems to unfit us for dealing with it. It is
possible, indeed, that the very fact that we so persistently think of it in financial or social rather than
individual terms is a symptom of our lack of understanding of its true nature, and that progress would
consist for us, not in better, but in less endowing
and organizing. Artistic salvation may lie, for us, in

183

the direction of giving due weight to individual effort, slow and intangible as it is, and of learning gropingly and patiently to understand its psychology. Nevertheless certain helps that can be given our music through intelligent financial and social arrangements are, despite their comparative superficiality, worth considering before we pass to the more fundamental question of how our personal efforts should be directed.

Broadly speaking, probably from eighty to ninety per cent of the endowments of our present orchestras, choral societies, and chamber-music organizations is spent on the performance of the great permanent musical classics. Since our whole musical civilization depends on the maintenance of standards of quality, this is as it should be, and we have no quarrel with it. But the other ten or twenty per cent, providing novelties and minor works, is almost entirely devoted to European music, much of it obviously mediocre and ephemeral, while not more than between two and five per cent, let us say, of this American capital is invested in American music. Why? First, because standards of choice are exotic and sophisticated; second, because music is regarded as an entertainment rather than as a spiritual adventure; third, because the importance of local loyalty, or intelligent provincialism, in building up contemporary art is not understood. If we were really interested in developing our own music, we should wish to give it more chance to be heard, not because we expected it to contain a larger proportion of masterpieces than German, or French, or any other contemporary music, but because it can grow only through experience, it can get experience only through us, and after all it is ours. Artistic curiosity is a fine thing; but, like charity, it begins at home. Germany has plenty of interest to support what the young Germans are doing, France to support the experiments of the French; why not save a little of our own curiosity for the young Americans?

Such an attitude on our part would be consciously tentative and experimental—at the opposite pole from spread-eagle chauvinism. Exorbitant claims made for our music in the propaganda of those who have commercial or other selfish reasons for "boosting" it do it incalculable harm. A musical journal, for instance, prints a list of fifty American works which it pronounces "thoroughly worthy of a hearing in company with *any* music," suggesting that one of them be placed on each program of the Philharmonic–Symphony Society during an entire season. Mr. Toscanini has avoided the music of his employers rather pointedly, but this is flying to the other extreme. The judicious know that there do not exist fifty such American works, that it is doubtful, indeed, if there exist fifty Russian or fifty English works of the level of merit indicated. This sort of thing cannot but alienate people of cultivated taste, who too often, alas, cease to take any interest at all in their own music. But the trouble is not in the music, but in the exaggerated claims made for it. Far more modest should be our claims. Some music we know we have already, quite good enough to appear on programs beside the contemporary music, neither better nor worse, of other countries. Since it depends on us for its chance to live (for even the most fanatic nationalist would hardly expect Europe to play our music before we do), let us hear it, and judge it, and give it discriminating criticism that may help it to improve.

The same principles of proportional expenditure of endowments that hold for orchestras and chamber-music ensembles would seem to apply also to less professional or permanent groups, such as music clubs, school and college orchestras, and music festivals. All might well make it a policy to give the American composer his chance, not because he has altogether arrived, but because he is hopefully on the way. A recent festival of chamber music, held in the very grounds of the national

Capitol at Washington, contained not a note of American music. A special feature of it was a work commissioned from Prokofieff. How much more constructive, one could not help thinking, would have been a commission to David Stanley Smith, or John Alden Carpenter, or Leo Sowerby, or John Powell, or indeed to any one of half a dozen of our own men!

One special field for endowments that might be of great practical aid to American composers may be pointed out here, since even our most generous benefactors have neglected it. Intelligent help might ease the financial burden of issuing serious works. The manuscript orchestral material for a symphony costs the composer from three to five hundred dollars to issue. If the work is played ten times (a highly liberal estimate) and if half the orchestras are willing to pay him fifty dollars rental fee for the material (which is unlikely, unless he already has a reputation), he will get back half his outlay. Meanwhile the manuscript orchestral parts will have been so marked up in black, blue, and red pencil with the conflicting phrasing and dynamic marks of the different orchestras as to be well-nigh illegible. Publication of such works is possible, outside of one or two commercial firms of unusual capital and high ideals, only through the Juilliard

Foundation, the Eastman School, or the Society for the Publication of American Music—all very generous in their financial arrangements, but hardly able to publish all the worthy works. Any endowment contemplated to help composers with either manuscript material or publication should be carefully based on actual performances by reputable organizations. No jury system can be relied upon to exclude unoriginal work in the current fashionable style, or technically well-written *Kapellmeister* music.

So much for endowment. As for organization, one of the most useful forms it can take is the making known of the best available American material to the groups most likely to play it. For orchestral music, for instance, there are Dr. Hanson's "List of Works Performed by the Greatest Number of American Orchestras during the Period 1919–1925," and our supplement carrying it down to 1930, both printed above in Chapter Two. While no exactly similar list exists for chamber music, a serviceable one may be compiled from the "List of Published Orchestral and Chamber Music Compositions by American Composers" which forms Appendix I of John Tasker Howard's *Our American Music*. If we select from the hundreds of works by a hundred and thirty composers there listed

188

the chamber-music compositions outstanding for
beauty, originality, and feasibility for professional
and amateur groups of ordinary technical skill, we
shall get something like the following

LIST OF CHAMBER-MUSIC WORKS BY AMERICAN COMPOSERS

Parker Bailey: *Sonata, flute and piano.* Society for
the Publication of American Music
("S.P.A.M.")

Cecil Burleigh: *Sonata, violin and piano, The Ascension.* Schirmer.

*Sonata, violin and piano, From the Life of
Saint Paul.* Carl Fischer

John Alden Carpenter: *String Quartet.* Schirmer

Sonata, violin and piano. Schirmer

George Whitefield Chadwick: *Piano Quintet.*
Schmidt

String Quartet No. 4, E minor. Schirmer

String Quartet No. 5, D minor. Schmidt

Frederic S. Converse: *String Quartet.* Schirmer

Sonata, violin and piano. Boston Music Company

Rubin Goldmark: *String Quartet.* Schirmer

Sonata, violin and piano. Breitkopf.

Trio, D minor. Breitkopf

Percy Grainger: *Mock-Morris, String Sextet.*
Schirmer

Walking Tune. Wind Quintet. Schott

Charles T. Griffes: *Two Sketches for String Quartet,
on Indian Themes.* Schirmer.

189

Henry Hadley: *Piano Quintet, A minor.* Schirmer

Howard Hanson: *String Quartet.* Birchard

W. C. Heilman: *Piano Trio.* S.P.A.M.

Edward B. Hill: *Sonata, clarinet (or violin) and piano.* S.P.A.M.

Henry Holden Huss: *Sonata, violin and piano.* Schirmer

String Quartet. S.P.A.M.

Edgar Stillman Kelley: *String Quartet.* Stahl

Daniel Gregory Mason: *Sonata, violin and piano.* Schirmer

Pastorale, violin, clarinet, and piano. Mathot

Three Pieces for Flute, Harp, and String Quartet. S.P.A.M.

Sonata, clarinet (or violin) and piano. S.P.A.M.

String Quartet, on Negro Themes. S.P.A.M.

Variations for String Quartet, on a Theme of John Powell. Oxford University Press

Fanny Blair. Folk-song Fantasy for String Quartet. Oxford University Press

Arne Oldberg: *Piano Quintet.* Summy

John Powell: *Sonata Virginianesque, violin and piano.* Schirmer

Sonata, violin and piano, A flat. Schirmer.

Arthur Shepherd: *Triptych, for High Voice and String Quartet.* S.P.A.M.

David Stanley Smith: *String Quartet No. 1, E minor.* Schirmer

String Quartet No. 3, C major. S.P.A.M.

String Quartet No. 4, E flat. Oxford University Press

David Stanley Smith: *Piano Quintet.* Oxford University Press

    Sonata, violin and piano. S.P.A.M.

    Sonata, violoncello and piano. Schirmer

    Sonata, oboe and piano. S.P.A.M.

Leo Sowerby: *Serenade for String Quartet.* S.P.A.M.

    Suite, G major, violin and piano. Boston Music Company

    Sonata, violin and piano. Universal Edition

Albert Stoessel: *Suite in Ancient Style, two violins and piano.* S.P.A.M.

Bernard Wagenaar: *Sonata, violin and piano.* S.P.A.M.

Emerson Whithorne: *Greek Impressions, for String Quartet.* Senart.

    Piano Quintet. Carl Fischer

This list, drawn from the entire territory of the United States (excluding only composers who, like Bloch and Loeffler, no matter how distinguished, are not representatively American) seems surprisingly short. If we ask why it is not longer, we find ourselves brought back to the point from which we started—the supreme importance of personal initiative. It is not longer because our composers have not made it so. It is the composers who, in the last analysis, create the musical culture of a country; their works *are* its music; endowments, organization, even the good taste of listeners, are all of secondary importance and cannot raise it to a

higher level than that of the composers. Institutions and organizations, in fact, are like the non-
combatant society at home in time of war. They
give necessary backing; they send food, arms, sup-
plies to the front; but it is the soldiers alone who
are on the firing line—and it is the composers who
are on the firing line of music. . . . Hence if our
music even today shows more promise than full
achievement, it must be because our composers fall
short in some of the essential qualities of great
artists. We have elsewhere attempted an analysis of
these essential qualities, finding them to include
independence, spontaniety, workmanship, originality, universality, and fellowship.[1] Are our American composers strikingly deficient in any of these?

The proverbial impatience of our national character leads most of us, it may be candidly confessed,
into a disastrous neglect of workmanship. The
technique of musical composition is one of the most
difficult, complex, intangible, baffling techniques
to be found in any of the arts. Even Beethoven
never fully mastered it, Schubert and Schumann
through their defects in it fell far short of their po-

---

[1] See *Artistic Ideals,* a book that may be considered as a more
important supplement to the argument of this one. Here we are
discussing chiefly the public and external aspects of American music,
while there the subject is the inner psychology of talent and character
that determines all artistic creation.

tentialities, César Franck attained only at sixty his full proficiency in it, Haydn, Wagner, and Verdi, "grand old men" of music, kept on conquering it right up to the end. Yet we Americans, with our haste, superficial "efficiency," and feverish itch for "results," think no shame to take correspondence lessons in harmony with the expectation of emerging finished composers. The amount of waste effort of this sort going on among us is pathetic—and exasperating. People try to write music who have scarcely learned to write words in intelligible sequence. People who cannot tell a sonnet from a simile will blithely embark on a sonata or a symphonic poem. People who are completely illiterate —in melody, harmony, form, orchestration—apparently spend a large part of their time competing for prizes in musical composition. It is such people who expect our already overworked orchestras to "encourage" them by reading over in rehearsal, from illegible manuscripts, their bungling efforts. This is to put the cart before the horse. In an interview telling how many such pieces are submitted to him for performance by the Los Angeles Orchestra, often showing marked talent, but usually no training whatever, Dr. Artur Rodzinski insists, with inspiring common sense: "The urgent need is greater facilities for the fuller development of

native talent. It is teachers we need, not performances of half-baked works."—Teachers, yes; but
even more we need the spirit of workmanship, the
resolve to learn, a little healthy stoicism and self-
help. So long as the young composer has access to
scores, to rehearsals, and to discussions with his
friends, all he needs in order to master his trade is
endless patience. Let him study, and study, and
study again. Success is earned not in the crowd, but
in laborious retirement.

As our American impatience too often defeats
us in the achievement of workmanship, so our long
habit of feeling inferior to Europe sorely impedes
our originality. This sense of inferiority, subtly and
subconsciously working, leads most of our young
men to accept as their conception of originality one
which is dubious even for young Europeans, inap-
propriate and disastrous for us. The cult of ugliness, disorder, disillusion, which may be a necessary phase for a Europe more than half effete, is
simply irrelevant to a young, vigorous, and idealis-
tic people like ourselves. How silly, and how piti-
able, are the third-rate Stravinskys and Schönbergs
so many of our young men make of themselves in
the search for a mistaken "originality"! The true
originality would be to turn our backs on all this
European degeneracy; to resolve to be ourselves; to

look about us at our own cheerful people, in our own grandiose, half-civilized scene, sparkling in our own keen atmosphere, and listen to the music that then spontaneously arises in us. One thing is certain: if our music is our own, it will not be disillusioned or cynical or sophisticated or ugly; it may be crude, and that at first will do it no harm; it will surely be active, energetic, and full of naïve humor and unashamed sentiment.

Finally, one hopes that, whatever its devotion to locality, its growing belief in the here and now from which all valid originality flowers, it will not adopt a narrow nationalism or lose its devotion to impersonal, supra-national beauty, on which depends universality. With our great material power, our wealth, our vast size, we have plenty of temptation to spread-eagleism, to the bumptious variety of patriotism that expresses itself in the chauvinist and the jingo. But "patriotism" of that egotistic, self-seeking sort is not to be confused with the Emersonian self-reliance in which we have been finding the root of originality. Art, like patriotism, begins with instinct and must always be rooted in it; but there is a natural evolution or ripening of instinct that it must go through if it is to reach true maturity and realize its highest possibilities. It must be spiritualized, broadened from its initial narrow

195

to the widest possible loyalty. True it is, as we are often reminded by the nationalists, that music cannot be vitally international or cosmopolitan unless it has begun by being sincerely national. The merely eclectic cosmopolitanism of the sophisticated intellectual, illustrated in so much contemporary European music, is still-born, never comes alive at all. But on the other hand jingo music, such as we hear in the perorations of patriotic overtures, never grows up. . . . It is to be hoped that our American music, after its timid, repressed childhood, may have first a lusty youth and then a kind, generous, intelligent maturity. That would be in our finest tradition, the tradition of Emerson and Whitman, who for all their ardent Americanism, and as its natural goal, were world patriots and lovers of the human race.

Such are some of the ideals our young composers may try to bear in mind if they hope to lead American music to a sounder workmanship, a simpler and truer originality, a wider universality, than it can show today. Is their hope destined to fulfillment? Who can tell? To some moods, we may as well admit, there seems little or no hope for American music. The obstacles seem too great: the indifference of our masses, the strangle-hold of European standards and conventions on the more intelligent minority, the difficulties of all kinds, economic, psychological, technical, emotional, and spiritual, that beset our composers. . . . In other moods we see that our music is already incomparably more vigorously alive than it was ten years ago—and we dare to hope. Whatever is to come, we may be sure that the most essential of all contributions to it is being made by the young composer who goes into retirement in order to perfect his own skill, to ripen his own art, thought, and feeling. The "hustlers," the organizers, the self-advertisers make, of course, far more noise than he; for the moment they seem to have all the power—and we all like power. But let him remember that it is not they, but he and his fellows, who are creating the fundamental values underlying our whole musical life. He can afford to leave them the present, he who has the most creative of all powers—the power to mold the future.

COMPLETING CHAPTER TWO

Lists of American works played by the Cincinnati, Cleveland, Detroit, Los Angeles, Minneapolis, and St. Louis orchestras during the five seasons 1925–6 to 1929–30.

FIGURE VII

CINCINNATI ORCHESTRA
American works played, 1925–30
(Asterisks indicate first performance anywhere.)

	1925–6
Ballantyne:	*From the Garden of Hellas*
Griffes:	*Poem for Flute and Orchestra*
	(Chalmers Clifton, guest-conductor)
Sowerby:	*Money Musk*
	1926–7
Carpenter:	*Adventures in a Perambulator*
	Concertino

199

Gershwin: *Rhapsody in Blue*
           Concerto for Piano and Orchestra

Hadley: *Symphony No. 3*

1927–8

Carpenter: *Skyscrapers*
Copland: *Scherzo for large orchestra*
C. Hugo Grimm: *Erotic Poem*
Stillman Kelley: *The Pit and the Pendulum*

1928–9

Gershwin: *An American in Paris*
Gruenberg: *Jazz Suite* *
Mason: *Chanticleer* *
Sowerby: *Ballade for Two Pianos and Orchestra*

Stillman Kelley: *New England Symphony*

1929–30

S. L. M. Barlow: *Symphonic Poem: Alba*
Hans Levy Heniot: *A Mountain Legend*
MacDowell: *Piano Concerto No. 2*
Sousa: *Two Marches*
           (John Philip Sousa, guest-conductor)

FIGURE VIII

CLEVELAND ORCHESTRA
American works played, 1925–30
(Asterisks indicate first performance anywhere.)
1925–6

Chadwick: *Tam O'Shanter*

An "All-American Program" was given under the direction of Dr. Howard Hanson, March 11–13, 1926, containing the following works:

Cooley: *Song and Dance,* viola and orchestra
Hadley: *Lucifer*
Hanson: *Lux Æterna*
Parker: *Cahal Mor,* baritone and orchestra
Schelling: *A Victory Ball*
Whithorne: *The Aeroplane*

The program of April 15–17, 1926, contained:

Douglas Moore: *The Pageant of P. T. Barnum*

and also an interesting analysis of the programs for the season. In this the following percentages are given:

German-Bohemian-Norwegian   40%
Russian-Finnish   20%
Italian-French   17.4%
Miscellaneous-Modern   22.6%

and under the last item is the note: "Of seventeen compositions, five were repeated from former seasons and twelve were played for the first time in Cleveland, of which eight were by American composers."

1926–7
Moore: *The Pageant of P. T. Barnum*

Schelling: *A Victory Ball* (twice during
                    the season)
Whithorne: *The Aeroplane*

                    1927–8
Borowski: *Semiramis*
Shepherd: *Horizons* *

                    1928–9
Griffes: *The White Peacock*
Hanson: *A Lament for Beowulf*
Herbert: *American Fantasy*
Whithorne: *New York Days and Nights*

                    1929–30
Elwell: *The Happy Hypocrite*
Griffes: *The White Peacock*
Janssen: *New Year's Eve in New York*
Kolar: *Symphony, D major*
Shepherd: *Horizons*

FIGURE IX

DETROIT ORCHESTRA
American works played, 1925–30
(Asterisks indicate first performance anywhere.)

                    1925–6
Carpenter: *A Pilgrim Vision*
Hadley: *Ocean*

                    1926–7
DeLamarter: *Organ Concerto*
Kelley: *New England Symphony*

202

1927–8

Carpenter:	*Skyscrapers* (Kolar)
Converse:	*Flivver 10,000,000* (Shavitch)
Mason:	*Symphony No. 1.*

1928–9

Kolar: *Symphony* (Kolar)

1929–30

Heniot:	*Mountain Legend* *
McKinley:	*Masquerade*
Mason:	*Chanticleer*
Wagenaar:	*Divertimento*

FIGURE X

LOS ANGELES ORCHESTRA
American works played, 1925–30
(Asterisks indicate first performance anywhere.)

1925–6

Hanson:	*Nordic Symphony*
McCoy:	*Prelude to "Egypt"*
Powell:	*Rhapsodie négre*
Sowerby:	*Money Musk*

1926–7
. . . .

1927–8
(Georg Schneevoigt, conductor)

Carpenter: *Skyscrapers*

1928–9

Dunn: *Overture on Negro Melodies*

Eichheim:	*Burma*
Hill:	*Stevensoniana, Suite No. 2*
Powell:	*In Old Virginia*
Deems Taylor:	*Through the Looking Glass*

1929–30
(Artur Rodzinski, conductor)

| Gruenberg: | *Jazz Suite* |

FIGURE XI

MINNEAPOLIS ORCHESTRA
American works played, 1925–30
(Asterisks indicate first performance anywhere.)

1925–6

Eichheim:	*A Chinese Legend*
Hanson:	*Nordic Symphony*
Schelling:	*Impressions from an Artist's Life*
	A Victory Ball
Sowerby:	*Suite: From the Northland*

1926–7

John Beach:	*The Asolani* *
DeLamarter:	*Symphony No. 2*
Hutcheson:	*Fantasie for Two Pianos and Orchestra*

1927–8

| Hanson: | *Pan and the Priest* |
| Schelling: | *A Victory Ball* |

204

1928–9

Collins:	*1914: Tragic Overture*
LaViolette:	*Penetrella*
Stringham:	*The Ancient Mariner*

1929–30

Borowski:	*Youth*
Farwell:	*Suite: The Gods of the Mountain*
Gershwin:	*An American in Paris*
Stringham:	*Symphony* *
Deems Taylor:	*Through the Looking Glass*

FIGURE XII

ST. LOUIS ORCHESTRA
American works played, 1925–30
(Asterisks indicate first performance anywhere.)

1925–6

E. R. Kroeger:	*Mississippi* *
Schelling:	*A Victory Ball*
Schneider:	*Sargasso*
Sowerby:	*Suite: From the Northland*

1926–7

Busch:	*The Song of Chibiabos*
Collins:	*1914: Tragic Overture*
Converse:	*The Mystic Trumpeter*
Schelling:	*A Victory Ball*
Whithorne:	*New York Days and Nights*

1927–8

Hanson:	*Pan and the Priest* (Goossens)

205

TUNE IN, AMERICA.

1928–9

Chadwick:	*My Jubilee*
Kroeger:	*Mississippi*

1929–30

Gershwin:	*An American in Paris*